165101

Jazz Greats Speak

Interviews with
Master Musicians

Roland Baggenæs

THE SCARECROW PRESS, INC.
Lanham, Maryland • Toronto • Plymouth, UK 2008

SCARECROW PRESS, INC.

Published in the United States of America
by Scarecrow Press, Inc.
A wholly owned subsidiary of
The Rowman & Littlefield Publishing Group, Inc.
4501 Forbes Boulevard, Suite 200, Lanham, Maryland 20706
www.scarecrowpress.com

Estover Road
Plymouth PL6 7PY
United Kingdom

British Library Cataloguing in Publication Information Available

Library of Congress Cataloging-in-Publication Data

Jazz greats speak : interviews with master musicians / [interviewed by] Roland Baggenæs.
    p. cm.
  Includes index.
  ISBN-13: 978-0-8108-5922-7 (pbk. : alk. paper)
  ISBN-10: 0-8108-5922-X (pbk. : alk. paper)
  1. Jazz musicians—Interviews. I. Baggenæs, Roland, 1937–. II. Coda magazine.
ML385.J196 2008
781.65092'2—dc22   2007052010

Printed in the United States of America

∞™ The paper used in this publication meets the minimum requirements of
American National Standard for Information Sciences—Permanence of Paper
for Printed Library Materials, ANSI/NISO Z39.48-1992.
Manufactured in the United States of America.

For Lasse and Sture and Thomasia

"It's just music. It's playing clean and looking for the pretty notes."

—Charlie Parker

Contents

Preface

*J*azz musicians usually tell their "stories" when they play their instruments. They share their feelings and thoughts with the listeners, and through their music they give one an insight into life, what life is about. It is often said, for instance, that Lester Young's music changed the life of many people. It did so because the great tenor saxophonist and clarinetist challenged one's intellect and confronted one's feelings. So did Charlie Parker, Louis Armstrong, John Coltrane, Billie Holiday, and a few others. I always felt that those great artists were speaking directly to me. Their music affected and moved me, and had and has that same magic impact on me as great classical music and the best literature.

Besides listening to the music, I always enjoyed hearing and reading the artists *talk* about their music. Since 1965, when jazz writing became a part of my professional life, I have met and interviewed a great number of jazz artists. The seventeen dialogues in this book were all previously published in the Canadian magazine *Coda* between 1972 and 1988. They are extensive, were done in a relaxed and pleasant atmosphere (no deadlines!), and unintentionally cover a good part of the history of jazz up to the late 1980s. The oldest interviewee was Benny Waters, born in 1902, and the youngest was Howard King, born in 1955. One of the artists, Marie-Ange Martin, is French, two are Danish (Pierre Dørge and John Tchicai), and fourteen are American. I believe the dialogues will speak for themselves, and I hope you will truly *listen* to them.

I would like to thank the musicians I interviewed—more than half of them, sad to say, are not with us any longer. First of all, though, I want to thank my son, Lasse, a musician and music teacher in his own right. Without his enormous help and great skills, this book would never have happened. Thanks also to Joel Dangiwa, Thorbjørn Sjøgren (who compiled the biographies at the beginning of each chapter), Jørgen Bo, Jan Persson, and Pelle Thomsen, to Frank Büchmann-Møller, Norbert Ruecker, and Allan Stephensen. Special thanks to my lifelong friend, Peter Sten Jacobsen, to Renée Camus of Scarecrow Press, to Edward Sanyang, and to Mariatu, who at the tender age of eleven is a unique friend and an inspiration.

Roland Baggenæs
The Gambia, West Africa

Dexter Gordon

$\mathcal{D}$exter Gordon (1923–1990) went on the road with Lionel Hampton's touring band at seventeen, and following periods with the big bands of Fletcher Henderson, Louis Armstrong, and Billy Eckstine, Gordon had by 1946 developed a bebop vocabulary for the tenor saxophone, originally inspired by Lester Young. After partnering with Teddy Edwards, Gene Ammons, and Wardell Gray, Gordon spent most of the 1950s in "correctional facilities" but enjoyed a notable comeback in 1961. From 1962 through 1976 he was based in Copenhagen, playing regularly in the famous club Montmartre. A second comeback and lucrative recording contract made him return to the United States in 1976, but his playing during the '80s never reached previous peaks. He had a leading role to much acclaim, acting as well as playing in Bertrand Tavernier's movie Round Midnight.

Would you tell about your motives for going to Europe in 1962?

Well, what happened was that I had come back to New York in 1962 and I was there for about six months. One night I met Ronnie Scott in Charlie's Bar. We knew of each other of course, and we talked, and he asked if I would be interested in coming to London and playing at his club. So I said of course, and he got my address and phone number. A few days later he called me and asked if such and such a time would be okay. He said that I'd work there for a month, including a tour around England, one night here and one night there. He also said that he would try to get some other things also over here on the Continent. So that meant two or three months of work. I was living in New York at that time, but I couldn't work there very much because they had that cabaret license thing going on, so anybody who had a narcotics record couldn't get a card, like Billie Holiday and a thousand others. Anyway, I came over and I guess I was in England for about five or six weeks. By that time Ronnie had contacted the famous club Montmartre in Copenhagen, and I went from London to Copenhagen in the fall. Actually, when I came I was six days late,

---

Previously published in *Coda*, June 1972

London being pretty open. This was my first visit to Europe and I had just planned to come over and do the tour.

You had no plans about staying over here?

Maybe subconsciously, but, no, it wasn't a permanent move. I still had my apartment in New York and I sublet it to a friend of mine. But it was certainly a big love affair with me and the Danes and vice versa, so I stayed at Montmartre for about a month and did a tour—Göteborg, Stockholm, and Oslo—and came back to Montmartre. And so this kept going on and on until finally, about two years later, I saw an article, I think it was by Ira Gitler, and he referred to me as the expatriate Dexter Gordon. And then it hit me and I said to myself—"Well, have I really been here that long?" But I was happy, everything was going nicely, and I had not been thinking in terms of time. But as it turned out it was a very good move—to me anyway.

We had not heard much of you during the '50s.

Well, I was addicted at the time and was in and out of jails. I was not playing so much, I mean it's such a terrible habit and it just takes up all your time. You're constantly looking and searching—you can still work but it's difficult, and of course they have very strong laws in the States about all this. So, consequently, in the '50s a lot of my time was spent in jails and hospitals, until finally, around 1960, I stopped. I'd had enough. I was tired because it didn't make sense. Before I came to Europe I had started recording for Blue Note. I made my first record in 1961 with Horace Parlan and another with Kenny Drew, Philly Joe Jones, and Paul Chambers. Around the same time I did this thing in Hollywood, *The Connection*, which is a story all about addicts. It's a very good play; the concept is very hip because they don't really preach a moral in the play. You just see more or less an average day in an addict's life, and everybody talks about experiences—da-da-da—and the band is on stage, and as I said they don't preach moral. I mean, it's up to you as an individual. Consequently, the whole concept is very realistic. I made the music and I think I recorded most of the things.

The play was performed in Denmark in 1964, and as I remember it, it did not turn out very successfully.

Very few people in Denmark had any idea of what the play was about. When the actors were performing and were supposed to be getting high, their reactions were as if they were drunk. They had no concept of how an addict reacts. I was the only one in there at that time who had any idea of what it should be like; not even the instructor knew. So I could only say once in a while that it was not quite . . . you know, but I wasn't the instructor so I couldn't really teach anybody. So the play ran for about five days. And another thing—like the actors, the audience had no concept of what it was about. Nobody could relate. But now today with so many kids doing the same thing or other things, they could be curious or become interested. Actually, the play was up again this year. I didn't have a chance to see it but they said it was good. But at that time nobody knew what was happening, which was funny in a way.

Having not been able to follow your musical career in the '50s, it was a very positive experience to hear you play live over here. Had you found some new kind of inspiration, or had you played like that all the time?

I think I had been playing more or less the same way. But as I said I was so limited and couldn't move around very much. I didn't record very much. In the early '50s I did some things with Wardell Gray and then there was a little pause, enforced pause. Later on I recorded an album for Duotone called *Dexter Plays Hot and Cool*. Then I recorded with Stan Levey, *This Time the Drum's on Me*, and made another album, *Daddy Plays the Horn*, both coming out on a label called Bethlehem. Kenny Drew is on *Daddy Plays the Horn*.

You played all over Europe. How do you find the response from the European audiences?

Fantastic, fantastic! In general I think that European audiences are very inspiring, very attentive—most audiences you play for really come to listen. They're drinking of course and are having a good time, but most of the people who come to the clubs or to the concerts come there to listen. American audiences are usually much louder—of course many go to listen to the music, but there is a difference. I like the European audiences. In fact, it's so different being here. An artist gets a lot of respect for being an artist, a musician, and it's not the same thing in the States. I mean, in the States people think that all musicians are nuts, dope fiends. They think that all artists are like that because their concept of life is all business, money. That's not everybody of course, I mean in general. Over here one of the most important things—and one of the biggest reasons for my being here—is that you do get that respect and that's important. I never had it before, well from a few people, but not in general.

I remember you for saying that you had become a local—at least in this country . . .

Well, at the particular time I said that it was the height of the beat thing and all the jazz clubs were trying to switch over to beat or rock—or they were closing.

The interest had not disappeared but it had waned. Everything you heard on the radio, every place you went to, everything was beat! Even Montmartre had it going, but I would say that over the last three years it has become better again. I think the kids who have grown up listening to the Beatles, etc., have become more mature in their taste so they want to hear more music and less noise. And then also what has happened is that a lot of people have started playing a sort of fusion, jazz and rock together you know, like some things I do. I think that's great because it's a little different. What the guys are trying to do now is to take the best from the beat thing and include it into their music, which is what Miles Davis and Cannonball Adderley and others are doing.

Even Lee Konitz used an amplifier.

Yes, I remember that but he sounded good on it. He wasn't trying to play beat or anything and he's one of the few who used the electric thing intelligently. Most of the cats I've heard who used electronics, it didn't do anything. But for him—because he's very light anyway, he's very fluent but not what you would call a strong player—for him it really added something. Sonny Stitt uses it but he didn't have it when he was here with the festival. For me, I never used it. I'm too lazy and then I feel like that I'm strong enough and that I don't have to. Also I think you lose that natural sound and to me that's almost everything, the sound, and I worked too long, too hard to get that sound to put it into some electronics.

Tell us about some of your other activities.

I have made some TV things and I made the music for a film, *Pornografi*, which is playing now. *Pornografi* was really the first film I was asked to make the music to. I didn't do all of it; they had several short sequences in that film and they had different music for all of these. They used music by H. C. Lumbye, and also a Danish group, Dr. Dopo Jam, did one. I wrote the theme and we did about four or five sequences. As far as porno goes, it was okay.

I guess this country has a reputation for its pornography.

Yeah, yeah, since Christine Jorgensen.

Speaking of her, I think William Burroughs relates to her in one of his novels. I wonder if you read any of Burroughs's books?

I read *The Naked Lunch* and something else, but I want to get back to him as I understand more or less what he's talking about. But he's writing about things in other terms, using another terminology.

In a conversation with Saul Bellow, Erik Wiedemann [noted jazz and literary critic] mentioned the fact that Burroughs' novel *Nova Express* had been translated into Danish, and that he [Wiedemann] had done the translation. To that Bellow suggested the possibility of having the book translated into English.

Oh, he did! Ha, ha, ha. Well, that was also kind of symbolistic. I had a friend who could understand Burroughs, while I couldn't understand really. But I'll have to go back to him.

Let's go back to music again. You told me that you had developed as a musician since you came to Europe. How was it and how is it playing mainly with European musicians?

Well, when I first came here it was pretty bad; it was heartbreaking. But then again, on the other hand, I think that helped to develop me because in the States there are so many good musicians, especially in jazz, that you don't have to worry too much about the music. I mean most guys you are going to play with either you know or know something about them. But when I came over here I didn't know anybody and I was appalled. The European rhythm sections were terrible; they had no concept really of what their function was. There were a few individuals here and there who had some idea of what they should be doing and so forth, but in general it was very sad. But I must say that in these last ten years the quality of music has gone up 200 or 300 percent. Here in Denmark we've got several young cats who are potentially great, beginning of course with Niels-Henning Ørsted Pedersen, and then we've also got Hugo Rasmussen and Bo Stief, two other bass players who can really play. The quality has gone up and I think it's due to the influx of all the American musicians coming in and thus giving the Danish musicians a chance to play with them and really learn. Because that's the only way you learn, by playing and associating with good musicians. I mean, you can't learn jazz out of a book. The only way is to play—and to listen of course. I hope my being here has contributed to the development. I have been teaching a little, but most of my teaching has been on the bandstand. I had a couple of students I worked with and then I taught at the school in Vallekilde, and all that seems to be paying off. There are some young musicians here in Copenhagen who I think in two or three years will be very, very good. Fortunately we have this club, Montmartre, where the American musicians play in Denmark. I never miss a concert if I can help it. And they usually come down to the club, so in that way I see the cats. Most of them I know anyway, but I also get a chance to meet the younger musicians who are coming up. I really think we are lucky to have the club. I have visited the States a few times since

1962, like going back to the source. I feel it's necessary to go back once in a while, and it helps me because it's taken a different turn over there, the free thing, you know . . .

Which is not your bag?

Well, I don't know, not free free. I always have played a little free here and there, but not in the sense they are doing it today. But I'm beginning to find it kind of interesting, some of it.

At one time you talked about Albert Ayler's playing. You don't like his music?

No. I could never make it. I like Archie Shepp, I like Ornette Coleman, I like Don Cherry. But for me, when a man is playing free it doesn't mean that he is just playing anything anywhere. You have to have some knowledge of your instrument, knowledge of music. And I never felt that with Ayler; he always sounded to me like he just had been playing about six months. He seemed to be a nice cat, but every time I heard him it was ridiculous to me. I only met him over here, I didn't know him in the States. No, it never sounded to me like he knew what he was doing. Shepp and Ornette and Eric Dolphy—they all knew what they were doing. They were playing outside but they knew where they were going, and I can accept that because not everyone can play like Charlie Parker. So the music is moving, and some of it is good and some of it is shit.

John Coltrane said in an interview that Lester Young and you were the musicians who had influenced him most. Which artists have influenced you?

Well, there are so many, but I would say Lester Young was probably my biggest influence. I think I jammed with him a couple of times, and once at Minton's Playhouse I jammed with Lester and Ben Webster. I was about twenty, I guess, and of course they were both my idols and I was scared to death. And that was at the time, 1942–43, when Minton's was in its heyday and Dizzy Gillespie, Thelonious Monk, Kenny Clarke, and all these people were playing there. Jazz was changing, was taking a big step, but like all big steps it was a gradual thing. At that time, Parker, Dizzy, Monk, and Bud Powell were experimenting. I was with Billy Eckstine's band, which was the first bop big band and all the cats were playing there—Gillespie, Art Blakey, Tommy Potter, Gene Ammons, Sonny Stitt, Leo Parker—so I was in a good school.

When John Coltrane developed as a musician around 1960, did you learn anything from him?

Yes, I did. Ira Gitler said it was like—he was referring to Coltrane and Sonny Rollins—he said that he could hear traces of both Coltrane and Rollins in some of my newer things. And he said it was like a man having money in the bank and then going to the bank to draw some interest—which is a good phrase. Because both of these cats and others too learned something from me, and I turned around and went back to the bank. In music, especially in jazz, I've learned something from trumpet players, piano players, drummers. But I would say that Lester Young was my big influence. What I liked so much about him was that he was always telling a story; everything was so poetic and fit together so well. I liked very much his *joie de vivre*—at that time anyway. Later on—when all the cats were playing his shit, like Stan Getz and all these people, and making a lot of money—he became very disillusioned, which is understandable. I think that's why he died, really; he got to a certain point and he felt that more should be happening for him. He was respected of course by musicians and others, but not by society. It was more or less the same thing with Parker—also, Lester's experiences with the army had a lot to do with his disillusionment. From Lester I also learned that the lyrics to the song you play mean something. I think knowing the lyrics—although I don't always know all of it—helps you understand the tune better because it has some meaning to what the tune is about.

Do you prefer playing clubs or concerts?

Actually, I prefer clubs, where you can relax and there's no real pressure, while concerts, you know, everything's got to be right.

When you played at Newport in 1970, you had come all the way from Europe and you just played a few numbers.

I just played two numbers and, well, I guess it's understandable because they had so many people there. But then again they had Ike and Tina Turner, and they played for an hour, and I played for fifteen minutes. I played "Boston Bernie" and then "Darn That Dream" and I played a long cadenza at the end of "Darn That Dream." I had a feeling that was about it because George Wein was on the side, pacing up and down. After Newport I played the Vanguard, I did some recordings, I went to Chicago and to Los Angeles to see my family, then to San Francisco and back to Chicago. Don Byas happened to be there and I played with Ammons and Sonny Stitt in Detroit. I was in the States for about two months trying to keep a full schedule. So I hope more or less to do the same thing this summer.

Your father was a doctor, and musicians would come to the house . . .

That's right. My father would take me down to the theaters, and in that way I heard a lot of the bands. I must have met Duke Ellington when I was about eight, nine years old. He came to the house a few times for dinner. Miles Davis suggested that all musicians should meet and go down on their knees and thank the Duke. I agree with Miles and I think the same thing about Louis Armstrong. I played with Armstrong's band in 1944 for about six months. It was no big musical experience as the band was kind of mediocre. The thing was that Louis was always the soloist and there was somebody else in charge of the band. In the '30s it was Luis Russell, and when I was in the band it was a tenor player, Teddy McRae. Pops wasn't really the bandleader; it was always like Louis Armstrong with this and that band, and in that way it's no real personal thing.

Before you play a concert or a set in a club, how much has been planned by you about the music you are going to play?

Concerts you have to plan because you can't stand on the concert stage and ask, well, what to play. Also concerts are so short you have to know what it should be. At the clubs I don't plan very much. There may be a couple of things you like to do, but there's no hurry and you can talk about it.

You started playing clarinet, and before you took up tenor you played alto. Have you taken up other instruments?

I *have* a flute. I haven't been working on it much, but soon I'm going to start working and that might make my music a little more interesting. I don't mean to play flute all night, but a few tunes here and there, a Latin thing or something like that. Like I said, I haven't been working on it for a while; for some reason I stopped. Been so busy with the saxophone—that's still a problem! About a month ago I was down at the club and there was a tenor player, Jesper Nehammer, down there. He had a soprano saxophone, and as I was feeling good enough I tried it. I enjoyed playing it and I might take it up. But I think it is difficult to find a good one and also to play it in tune. The embouchure is more like playing clarinet. When I practice, most of the time it's working at scales and etudes and I find it very necessary. It's good too because I don't really get too much of a chance to read music any more. So it helps to keep my eyes together, like next week I will be going to Switzerland for about two weeks to play with an all-star big band, and so I'll have to be reading.

Do you listen to the young musicians?

Oh yeah, sure. And like I said there are several young cats in town who are really good. So I'll have to practice a little more! Jesper Nehammer, Palle Mikkelborg, and a fantastic pianist, Thomas Clausen. Mads Vinding, a young bass player, and a drummer, Kasper Winding, who is only about fifteen or sixteen and who is going to be great. I mean, it's beautiful to hear and it just seems that the last few months all these cats have started to blossom. I think the reason, the main reason, for that is the influence of the many American musicians living here, and also because we have the club. The club seems to be driving again after a few not-so-good years. Recently they had two months with almost every jazz musician playing without being paid—that's really free music! And everybody went for it.

Many people talk of a new trend in jazz these years represented by artists like Miles Davis, Herbie Hancock, Wayne Shorter, etc. Do you regard their music as a new kind of jazz?

Well it's different, but not necessarily new. These musicians all know what they're doing so it has a format. I'm not too sure of what that is, but there is a format. I heard Herbie Hancock the other week at Montmartre and it was very good. The band has been together for at least two years now, so everything they do is very tight.

Pharoah Sanders?

I worked opposite him at the Vanguard. His group at that time was not as good as Herbie's group. He had some younger cats who weren't really world-class at that time. Maybe today they are fantastic. Unlike Herbie's thing, which is still American—the contacts, the flavor, everything—Pharoah's thing is different, something like Yusef Lateef's concept. Sanders found much inspiration in the music of India, Asia, and Africa, but one night at the Vanguard he played blues. I don't know why, but he sounded like Stanley Turrentine, which was a surprise to me. I had worked opposite him for two weeks and every night it was the same flavor, but this particular night they went into that blues thing and that was interesting.

Have you listened much to the music of India, Asia, etc., and have you found inspiration from these cultures?

No, I haven't really listened, but I think Pharoah and those cats, I don't know whether it's religious or cultural or what. . . . Coltrane was getting into it, too.

He was into some kind of religion and therefore he was getting interested in other cultures, and this came out in his music. Myself, I'm into a HOF culture! [HOF, a Danish beer. R.B.] Of course, I've heard some of these people, but I haven't really related to it yet.

Are you politically involved?

Politically involved? Yes—ban the bomb!

Also referring to your album, *The Panther*, is it a political panther?

It's up to you. That's why I just named it *The Panther* instead of pink or black. I just left it open, but I guess in reality it refers to the Black Panthers.

Many musicians coming up today feel they must use their music also as a means of changing society . . .

I feel it's always been like that, consciously or subconsciously. I don't feel it's necessary to make speeches. To me music is such a personal thing; everything in your life is coming out in your music. You can't really eliminate social and political views from your music—it's in there.

You know what happened to Charlie Haden recently in Lisbon?

I was there. What happened was that Charlie Haden—he was there with Ornette Coleman, of course—dedicated this particular tune to all the oppressed black freedom fighters in Angola and Mozambique—and he did that in Lisbon! And that was fine and the audience gave him a big hand, just for the speech. It wasn't that long, just like we're playing this tune, da-da-da, and we're dedicating it to all the freedom fighters in Mozambique and Angola, da-da-da. So the next morning they were leaving to go to London and security people came to the hotel, but they had already left for the airport. So they called the airport and had them held, and I think they kept Charlie overnight or something. I can't remember.

The future?

I would like to write a little more. I've been thinking about it lately—getting more active into composing and arranging, so perhaps it comes . . .

· 2 ·

Marie-Ange Martin

Marie-Ange Martin (b. 1948) started playing guitar as a teenager and became interested in jazz after listening to records by Django Reinhardt, who became her main influence, and to gypsies playing in clubs in Paris. In the early '70s she played occasionally with American saxophonist Benny Waters, with whom she also went to Scandinavia. During the '70s she worked in small clubs in Paris, also playing cello and banjo. She visited Los Angeles in the '80s and met and played with American guitarists, among them Howard Roberts and Tal Farlow. In the '90s she worked with French guitarists Christian Escoude and Frederic Sylvestre and the accordion player Marcel Azzola, and did a tour with them through Eastern Europe, Asia, Australia, Indonesia, and Israel. She has recorded under her own name and with Sylvestre and Martin Gerard Siffert.

When I was thirteen years old I bought a guitar, and from a book I learned the chords and tried to learn to play some songs. Actually, I took up the guitar because I liked some rock groups; The Shadows was one of them. I don't like that kind of music now, but at that time I wanted to play that way. Later on I met a man who played not only jazz but also musette music, which is usually played on an accordion. It is very difficult to play on the guitar, but I learned to play some waltzes. One day I went to the Marche aux Puces, which is a big place in Paris. In some of the pubs there you can hear gypsies play, and I listened to them and kept coming back. My parents didn't want me to go there, but instead of going to school on Saturday afternoons I took the train to Paris and was able to stay just twenty-five minutes listening before I had to go back. I didn't bring my guitar and just listened, but they noticed me. I watched them and really listened, and when I came home I played what I had heard.

Did you go to a teacher?

No, except for the man who taught me the musette I had no teacher. However, two and a half years ago I began to learn the cello and also to read music.

Previously published in *Coda*, October 1972

Before that I only played by ear, and even now I play by ear. My interest in jazz began when I met these gypsies. After school I moved to Paris, took a little room, and began to work very hard with the guitar.

Did you listen to records at that time?

When I lived with my parents I didn't, as they had no record player. Later on I listened to Django Reinhardt's records and also to other jazz musicians. In fact, it has been only a year and a half since I began to know older jazz: King Oliver, Coleman Hawkins, Duke Ellington, and Count Basie. Also I had never heard Louis Armstrong before then.

How did you meet Benny Waters?

It was six months ago. I used to play with our pianist, Philippe Baudouin, who knows a lot of musicians in Paris. One time their usual guitarist and banjoist was not free, so I came to play with Benny. Since then I have played with him on some occasions, not very regularly. Two or three weeks before Benny had to go to Denmark, his bass player said he couldn't go, so Benny asked me would I like to go.

How would you describe the music of the New Orleans Middle Jazz Quartet?

It's very difficult for me. The pianist, Philippe, knows everything, while I don't know anything compared to him. I like the drummer, Al Craig, very much—he really swings. And Benny, I find him fantastic. We can say that he sometimes moves too much and does things to please the people, and I understand if someone tells me that he moves too much. As for myself, I always love him when he does it. And when he plays ballads on the tenor, it's always new ideas. I like to work with the group. I think that in some years I'll be playing more modern, but I have much work to do first. Playing with Benny, it's not very modern, but sometimes I try to play in a more modern style. I like to play bop and I have begun to learn some of Charlie Parker's themes with a young French saxophonist. Maybe sometime next year we'll form a small band.

When I read about the group you play with now I was surprised . . .

Because I'm a woman?

Not only that, but one might expect you, being so young, to be playing in a rock group or in a more modern jazz combo.

Well I'm not so young, and the great influence for me is really Django. It's not that I learn and try to do the same, but I've learned with gypsies and it's like that.

Those gypsies knew Django; they played with him and play in the same style. I am beginning to know some of the younger jazz musicians, but so far I haven't met or played with any of the American jazz musicians who live in Paris.

You play guitar and cello.

I've begun to learn cello, but it's very difficult. I have been playing it for two and a half years and maybe I need ten years; it's not like the guitar. It is not more difficult, but you have to work every day. My guitar is a copy of a Selmer built by Fauino. I would like to get a Gibson, but because I don't work too much I'm not able to buy one now. On my guitar I'm not able to play more modern because of the sound.

Do you enjoy working in clubs?

Yes, if I don't play in the evening I miss it. In France, though, the young people don't like jazz, and I don't like when we go into a club and play three sets a night and between sets people listen to loud pop music. They don't like our music and it is not very satisfying if the audience doesn't like what you do. Here the audience is very nice and I was surprised that the young people knew about jazz so well and also that they knew the words of the songs.

Do you communicate a message with your music?

Oh, no. I play because I like it. I have nothing to tell. Somebody told me that my playing was for the liberation of the woman or something like that, but no. I'm not interested in any of these movements. As I told you before, I never read newspapers and never listen to the radio, also I never vote. Maybe it's wrong, I don't know. Also, I never think about my music as being a part of a European culture or being influenced by other cultures. I am never thinking that way. Maybe sometimes I take something from here and from there and put into my music. And when I listen to a record, it's not for one day; it is for one or two weeks.

Have you composed anything?

I haven't so far. I think I will when I have my own band in some years. The most important thing for me now is to get a style. For the moment everybody says, "Oh, you've heard Django and a little Charlie Christian and probably you like Barney Kessel." And it's true; every time I listen to other guitarists, I go back to Django. I shall not play like that all the time, but I feel a great love for Django. Also I like Charlie Christian, Wes Montgomery, Barney Kessel, Joe Pass, Kenny Burrell, and George Benson. Probably I have forgotten some names. And going back to Django, he had so much imagination, so many ideas. He could play very fast but also he could play just two notes that would make you listen.

This is your first visit to Denmark?

Yes, it's the first time I've been outside France except for three weeks in Liverpool as a schoolgirl. I think people here are very nice, and the family that got us here is, well, they are very kind. I went to the club in Copenhagen, Montmartre, and it was free jazz when I was there—Don Cherry. I liked the music when they were playing the themes, but I found the choruses too long.

How much do you know of the contemporary jazz scene?

Not much. It's not that I don't want to know, but I guess I need a few years. I like to start at the beginning. King Oliver, Louis Armstrong, Fletcher Henderson, Duke Ellington, Count Basie. And Charlie Parker—I like his music very much.

Would you like to teach?

No! In jazz, each musician has his way of playing. Some guitarists can tell me that I don't do that well, and that it would be better if I put my fingers like that. . . . But I do my way and they do their way, and I don't want to teach anybody my way.

The future?

I just want to go on and play guitar and play jazz all my life. That's the most important thing for me . . .

· 3 ·

Stanley Clarke

Before switching to double bass, Stanley Clarke (b. 1951) had played accordion, violin, and cello, and at twenty he had been on the road with Horace Silver and Joe Henderson. In Stan Getz's quartet he met Chick Corea, and in 1972 he joined Corea's Return to Forever group, with which he gained international exposure and fame, winning awards on both acoustic and electric basses. After leaving Corea in 1976 when the group turned to fusion, Clarke, accordingly, emphasized his use of the electric bass and often played in joint projects with George Duke. Since the mid-'80s he has switched back and forth between leading his own bands and participating in various all-star-like projects with Sonny Rollins, McCoy Tyner, Wayne Shorter, Jean-Luc Ponty, and others. Clarke has also been writing music for movies and for TV.

I come from a musical family. My mother sang in church choirs and things like that, so I was surrounded by music. She liked the music and bought a lot of records, so I listened to a lot of jazz, Duke Ellington and Count Basie and Stan Kenton, those types of things. I really liked them and I still do. The decision to become a jazz musician was mine. I don't know whether I necessarily had the idea of becoming a jazz musician. It just happened that, for me, playing what is called jazz music was the only way I could really play and express myself in some kind of way, and also make some type of living. When I was younger I started out playing violin. You see, I've always had very large hands and I couldn't quite get the fingering for that instrument. I played cello after that, and then I finally got to the bass and I guess the size of the instrument attracted me to it. The difference between the Fender and the "real" bass is that one bass is made out of wood and it has a more natural sound. The other bass is made out of steel and it's made to be used through electronic things, like amplifiers. And that has, I guess, a more synthetic sound. I personally like both of the sounds—they both fit in different situations. There are situations where the Fender bass fits better, and vice versa.

Previously published in *Coda*, June 1973

I listened to a lot of Jimmy Blanton, and I love what he did—I agree with you as far as him revolutionizing the role of the instrument. I think that I'm correct in saying that he was one of, if not the first, bass player to get away from just mainly being a timekeeper. I'll have to say that around Blanton's time, or after, Oscar Pettiford was really for me one of the most important bass players because he did what Jimmy Blanton was doing. He really could play bass solos and make a whole thing out of it. He was very good and he communicated to a lot of people. And after Blanton, much after Blanton, there were other important bass players, like Paul Chambers. He at times made the bass sound like a horn, in other words he made the bass sound like a saxophone, and sometimes he would play saxophone lines. He was very good also.

I think the possibilities are very good for me working as just a musician—playing in whatever situation is put upon me, playing whatever I have to do or whatever I want to do. And I basically just want to play beautiful music and communicate something to somebody, some happiness, some truth. And whatever you want to call it, I guess it's up to you, the audience. I really don't try to label music that I have played or will play. When I was coming up, rock was the present thing, so I listened to it. When I was learning how to play and becoming a musician, for some reason I could always play that. It didn't seem to be anything, to learn how to play rock, it didn't seem like it was anything. I get inspiration from a lot of things. Not necessarily. . . . See, I don't look at them as categories like art forms, literature, films, etc. I can get inspiration from anything. If I walk outside and it's a beautiful day, that will make me want to play. Or if I'm just around people I like to play with, that gives me inspiration. The things that really inspire me to anything are just basic things, like happiness, truth, and love, and things like that. Real African rhythms with drums give me a good feeling. I've always liked to listen to African music. So I guess if that's inspiration, that's what inspires me.

What do you feel could be done to make the situation better for jazz and its musicians as far as economics, chances of having the music exposed, etc., are concerned?

I know a lot of musicians who play very well, play their instrument very well, but they don't know too much about themselves. They live very loosely and it's very hard for them to progress economically, or even have their music exposed. There are a lot of musicians who just play their instrument and that's it. Which is cool, to an extent, if that's all you want to do, just play. But if you want your music to be exposed, you have to do other things, which I'm sure you know if you think about it.

How do you regard your function as a bassist in a band?

First of all, I like to break the whole sound thing into levels. So you have a bass player, someone who's playing the bass and keeping the time. And below that you have the drummer, and above that you have the chords, which may be a piano player. Then you have a horn player or whatever playing a melody. That's where the bass fits in. And of course that varies according to what situation you are in or who you are playing with. I've played in some bands where there's really no need for a bass player to play the role of a bassist, so you could play things that a horn would play. It all depends on the concept, whatever somebody's trying to do. To give you an example, in the band I'm playing with now, Return to Forever, I basically play the role of a bass player and a timekeeper. But then I can also play other roles. I can play chords and I can play like a guitar or something, different things. I think that whole thing is left up to the individual, how he wants to play the bass, what his idea is of a bass player. In other words, what he thinks the bass should sound like.

My first chance to hear you in person was at the 1972 Newport Festival in New York. What did that festival mean to you?

I liked playing at the festival. I got to play with a lot of musicians and I got to see other bands that I hadn't seen in a long time due to traveling and things like that, so that was good. As far as the festival meaning something to me, I'll have to say that the only thing it really meant to me was that everybody was supposed to have a good time and play some good music. Also I think the festival was set up in a way where a lot of people could get out to hear a lot of music. I hope that was the main purpose of the festival, to get the music out there.

You have been working with many different bands—bands that have completely different kinds of expression. Do you feel any conflict playing with, say, Stan Getz one day and Pharoah Sanders the following day?

No, I don't feel any conflicts. What I do in order to feel good doing these different things is to make myself able to change. Which is something I think all of us should be able to do—doing anything, even something other than music, and being able to change. If you can change and still feel good about it, it all feels good. Basically I play almost the same with Stan as with Pharoah Sanders. I play the same notes; it's just the concepts that are different.

Tell us something about the New York jazz scene, the record companies, the clubs, and the audience . . .

Well, I'll start out with what you can call the jazz scene. Personally I haven't felt too much of the jazz scene here in New York because I travel a lot. I remember there was a time when the musicians were more together. There were places where the musicians would go and play in what we call lofts. But they don't have too much of that any more. As for record companies, let me just say that a lot of those I've come in contact with are out to make some money and they're out to control somebody.

The club thing here in New York, from what I see, is pretty bad. First of all, there aren't that many clubs where you can play in New York, and the physical condition of the clubs keeps going down and down and down. At times it becomes very depressing to play in these clubs. A lot of the club owners in New York are nice, but there are also many bad ones. When I say bad club owners, I mean a lot of them are stuck-up about so-called jazz musicians. They think that a jazz musician only makes this amount of money and that he does this and he does that—meaning that jazz musicians always play on an out-of-tune piano or something like that. A lot of times the club owners don't have their equipment in order, meaning pianos, sound systems, and microphones. Of course, there are also nice club owners who have nice clubs and things.

As a musician you can have a good audience or you can have a dead audience; it really all depends. It has a lot to do with the musicians themselves. If I go to a club and I see musicians who are playing but not trying to communicate anything or not trying to put out some type of flow to the audience—I always find that the audience completely turns off and becomes very cold. It's a natural thing because when people come to a club, they want to go out feeling better than they did when they came. If I go to hear some music, I want to come out feeling lifted in some kind of way. And if I don't get lifted, I just get a very uneasy feeling.

Do you feel any limitations about playing in a recording studio compared to playing in a club?

I basically feel the same playing in a studio or in a club; just the overall feeling is there. The only difference is that I can play longer in a club. I can get a chance to play a tune and stretch out more, do more things with it, experiment more. But as far as limitations, I try never to feel limited in any way whatever I do. I just try to always play and feel free to do what I think is best for the actual situation.

So far, the great innovators of jazz have been black musicians . . .

I'll agree with you by saying that many of the great innovators have been black musicians. However, white musicians have always been involved, but for reasons that I just don't understand they've only recently been recognized. But, as I said, they've always been involved in the music.

Do you feel it is necessary for a young musician to have a certain knowledge of earlier periods of jazz, to go back to Armstrong and Bechet, to name just two?

I personally don't feel that it is necessary for a young trumpet player to study all Louis Armstrong's licks in order to play. That just doesn't sound logical. But I think that a young musician should be aware of what Armstrong did, which is not too hard because they will always be playing Louis Armstrong's music on the radio. Myself, I'll always hear it and I'll always love it. I think that a musician, young or old, if he has something to say musically, he's going to say it because *he*'s creating it, it's coming from *him*. It really has nothing to do with the past, because if it does I believe that it's a lie. I don't like to imitate somebody. If I'm playing a tune and Paul Chambers played the same tune, I'm not going to play it like he played it. Because I'm not Paul Chambers; I'm Stanley Clarke. So I'll try to play it the way I know how to play it in that situation.

You have just come back from Europe. Do you have any comments on the European musicians, the audiences, and the clubs you played in?

I like Europe very much and the people over there; it's different from where I'm from. It's a much easier pace, slower, and I really liked the audiences in Europe, especially in London. You see, I had a certain picture of English audiences, but when we were there we had a very good audience. Actually, everywhere we have been the people have accepted our music and really enjoyed it. I didn't play too many clubs. I played the Montmartre club in Copenhagen, and that was OK. Then I played at Ronnie Scott's in London, and like I said that was nice—I really enjoyed it.

Most of the young musicians today come out with an extensive musical and technical background. Do you think that makes them better jazz musicians, and do you think playing jazz and improvisation can be taught?

I'd say that the young musicians today come out with a better technical background than before because there are more places where you can go and learn an instrument for nothing. It's part of the whole school system. If your musical awareness is very high, you'll be a good musician regardless of how much technique you have. If you're able to spot a melody, just to play a melody, it doesn't matter how much technique you have. For me, the highest quality music is melodic music, music with pretty melodies. When I hear somebody play a pretty melody and then improvise off that melody and play other pretty melodies, that really knocks me out. I think that's a fantastic thing to do.

I really don't know what a jazz musician is. With a very high musical and technical awareness, it's only logical it's going to make you a better musician. A good musician to me is one who can play, improvise, play melodies, and play other things—one who can play far-out music or play on one chord, one who can play anything. To me, that's what a good musician is—someone who can do anything that has to do with music, or at least most of the things. And do I think playing jazz and improvising can be taught? Yes, it can be taught on a technical level—and I'll leave it at that.

Years back jam sessions were an almost everyday occurrence. How much still exists of the jam session thing?

Well, they still have what you call jam sessions, but it's not as much as it was once. I mentioned to you earlier about the musicians playing in lofts. They still do, but it's very scarce. Every now and then somebody might call me and say, "Let's get together and play." It's not an everyday thing, though; it only happens when a group of people all feel like doing it.

Who are, in your opinion, the most important figures in jazz right now?

I would say everyone who's in jazz right now, everyone who is in that—whatever that is—is an important figure. To me, everybody and everything is important, anybody who's doing something is important on some level.

I'd like to speak about the music of Return to Forever. I think the music is very simple music, meaning it's very easy to listen to, very easy to experience. Just to get into what I'm trying to say, there's a lot of music that you might find very hard to listen to and experience—it might make you feel funny or something. The music of Return to Forever makes *me* feel good when I listen to the playbacks or to our first album. Playing with the band in clubs or at concerts, I get a really good feeling. It's really inspiring, it lifts me. . . . The music is very light, but I don't want to go into the techniques of the music. If you want to analyze it, it's up to you what you want to do with it. The musicians in the band are Chick Corea, who plays both acoustic and electric piano, Joe Farrell, who's playing the reeds, Airto Moreira, who's playing drums, Flora Purim, who's singing and playing percussion, and myself.

To understand the philosophy behind the name, Return to Forever, I'll have to start out by defining what that name is: return meaning we're going back to something and forever meaning a place with no time and no end.

I believe there was a time when people—or whoever was here—felt very free. There was a time when there was a lot of happiness and freedom and that was a long time ago, a really long time ago. That was before anything. I believe there was a type of free civilization. And what we're trying to do is to return through our music. We try to get that feeling, that free feeling. For instance, when I play, I don't have any considerations about time. I feel it's never going to end. And when it ends, it's when it's supposed to end. I believe in doing a cycle of actions. You start something and you end it. And just that whole Return to Forever trip is like a thing that's just started. But we plan for a lot of good things to happen to the band. It's such a great feeling, a neverending feeling.

This group, Return to Forever, will be together until we're not together any more. The whole concept of the band will always be very high on my list. I'll always try to live by that, because it's something we have agreed upon. It's something that's real to us, this whole thing of feeling good while you play—always. When something doesn't feel good we get it out. Or something happening right in the band, which could be something that might be with the music, or something personal, we get it out. We tell the next person, we make it known, we communicate. And it always clears up, it always works. I'm sure all the great musicians have experienced it. You're playing with some people you like playing with, and you get this feeling you're not even on this planet and you're not thinking of time. The whole concept of time is not there. I personally believe that time is a lie. It's just something man has made in order to break his life up into cycles. It's a very easy thing to say—"I'll do this for an hour." More so than "I'll do this until I've finished it." I'm not saying time is bad. I think it's very good, but it's nice getting away from it. So you can do something and you start it and you finish it. It can take a minute and it can take days, and it's a very free feeling.

Are electronics being misused in jazz today, and what do you feel they add to your own playing?

No, I don't think electronics are being misused. If a guy is playing electric piano, is he misusing it? An electric piano is something that's supposed to be played and it's just there and it's just a piece of equipment. If you like the way Chick Corea plays the electric piano and you don't like the way Herbie Hancock plays the same instrument, I don't think you can say that Herbie Hancock is misusing the electric piano. About my own playing and my own use of electronics, I think all it adds is just colors, certain other kinds of textures. For instance, playing the Fender bass with a guitar player playing a certain type of music just sounds better with the electric bass. There's more presence in it for that thing; it usually has to do with volume.

If we accept the thesis that music, like other art forms, is to a certain degree a reflection of what is going on around us, what is it in society that forms the basis of the new and more melodic type of jazz coming up these years—played by groups like Return to Forever, Weather Report, Herbie Hancock's band—compared with the free jazz of the '60s with its more militant and harsh attitude?

Well, these groups that you mention are playing melodic things. I think that's just what the musicians are feeling. They're playing the type of music they want to play. As far as society is concerned, and I'll have to speak for myself, for Return to Forever, because I don't know too much of the other two groups, we try not to be the effect of whatever is happening in society. Because in this world, in society or whatever you want to call it, it's chaotic, it's totally insane. There's a lot of insane people in this world and I really think that to play music that reflects on society is nowhere. I think it's an endless cycle that doesn't go anywhere. Nothing happens. In other words, there's a lot of insane people you know of, a lot of people who are in power, who have a lot of power. And for me to go and play some music that reflects upon them, I would be playing insane music. So what I'm trying to do is play some music that communicates to some people, communicates some kind of truth, some happiness. I want to play some music that will make people happy, and once people are happy, when they are feeling good, they see more. I've experienced this myself.

I used to play a lot of free music when I was in college, so-called free jazz, and I used to feel bad. I used to go out and read the papers a lot and watch TV, watch the news, and read about Nixon and all that. And this wasn't too long ago and I used to get very drugged about this and play some really far-out music. What you call militant, harsh music. Just recently I got the feeling that I wanted to communicate some happiness to people, because it doesn't have to be the other way. All people aren't that way, all people aren't harsh, all people aren't insane. It's just that most people seem to be that way. All I want to do is to do what I'm doing now, and so I'll have to say that I don't think the music comes from society. I think this music comes from within, comes from the individual. Something they're feeling, some flow they want to put out to society. In other words, they want to be the cause and they want to get something out to some people and have them become the effect of this. I personally believe that an artist, at this point in time, should be a cause to the people. In this world somebody's always causing something and somebody else becomes the effect of that. To make things a lot better, an artist should take responsibility of being a cause, then the effect that comes out won't be as hard and militant. Basically, artists really are closer to the real truth than anybody on this planet. Anybody who's artistic, anybody who's creative, doing anything, and I don't care what it is, is closer to the truth than the normal cat in the street. So I think the artist should be the cause rather that being the effect of something. For me, it just doesn't sound right to play something that reflects what Nixon thinks.

You are featured on several records. Which do you prefer?

I like the record I did with Joe Henderson. It's called *In Pursuit of Blackness*, and it's on the Milestone label. I like the music we played on it. I like a lot of it and I felt good playing it. There's a record I did with Pharoah Sanders called *Live at the East*, and a lot of the music there was nice, very nice. I like the record I did with Chick, and we did another while we were in London, which came out in February. I did some records that haven't been released. There's a record with Stan Getz along with Chick Corea, Tony Williams, Airto Moreira, and myself. The music on that one is really powerful. I think it is probably the best album Stan ever made. I did a record for Dexter Gordon with Hank Jones playing the piano, Thad Jones playing trumpet, Louis Hayes playing the drums, and Dexter and myself. I really enjoyed that, and I must say that out of all the records I have made this one felt special. It was peaceful, and I love Hank Jones. He's such a beautiful person, and the way he plays is just like the way he is. He is a real gentleman. I would like him to be my father. Nothing to say against my real father, but I'd like to have a father like Hank Jones. Yes, he's really a nice person. There are some other records I like, and let me just mention one I did with composer and guitarist Luiz Bonfa.

Have you done any compositions or arrangements, or do you plan to do so in the future?

I have three compositions of mine recorded. One is called "Quiet Afternoon," and it was recorded by tenor saxophonist Buddy Terry on the Mainstream label. I think that was the first tune anybody recorded of mine. The second tune was recorded by a drummer named Norman Connors on the Cobblestone label. This tune is called "Blue" and I like the way that came out. And then, on the second album with Return to Forever, we recorded a tune of mine called "Light as a Feather." I was really happy how that came out. As far as plans for the future, I'm planning on doing my own album at the end of December and I hope it will be out in February.

How important is the close contact with the audience to you?

I think it's very important; I think it's the number-one thing on the list for me as far as playing and performing. When I'm performing, in order for the performance to go well, between the audience and myself there has to be no space. In other words, I'm going to put something out to them, and if I put it out strongly enough I'll get something back. That's my way of seeing it and feeling it, and that's the only way to get your music out there—to put it out to someone with some intention. And the intention has to be a truthful one, and at this point of my life, and probably always, the only real basic intention for my music is to make somebody feel good, feel better than they did before I played. When I get compliments, what I like to hear and really treasure are when people say that they heard me playing and that made them feel good and lifted them.

What will you be looking for musically in the time to come?

I'll have to say that I'm always looking straight ahead and that I just want to play some more beautiful music, some more music that will make people feel happy. And whatever form the music's going to make remains to be seen. Not to make it sound mysterious, but it's hard for me to say to you or try to explain to you what my music is going to sound like ten years from now. I just know it's going to sound good and that it will make some people feel happy.

Duke Jordan

After playing with Al Cooper's Savoy Sultans, Coleman Hawkins, and Roy El-dridge, among others, Irving "Duke" Jordan (1922–2006) was discovered by Charlie Parker in 1947, adding his distinctive, lyrical touch to Parker's legendary quintet and sextet recordings. Though also performing and recording with Sonny Stitt, Art Farmer, and Cecil Payne, his career until the early 1970s was rather erratic. He was rediscovered in 1973 and had lost none of his qualities, and for more than twenty years he continued to record and tour extensively, mainly in Europe and Japan. From 1978 until his death he lived in Denmark.

Duke, how is your musical situation right now?

Well, my musical situation right now would be that I'm all out, so to speak, and trying to catch up as much as I can as far as dexterity is concerned, contacts are concerned, old friendships, musical knowledge. . . . Because there are lots of old friends that if I'm lucky enough to run into them and I have any questions about music that I don't understand—if I ask them and they have the knowledge—they'll tell me or show me. So far as the musical situation right now, that's about it.

I have been playing with my trio here in New York at the Cellar for five weeks. You see, they had us from Sunday to Tuesday and they had us from Wednesday to Saturday. They kept switching us around, and then finally they had us there for the whole week. Now we're finished there, so we go somewhere else.

You have been out of music, away from the scene for some time.

Yes, a good five years. I got disgusted because I took my tunes and put them with a publishing company, and I found out that this company was stealing all my money and telling me "Well, this is all the money you have." But then

Previously published in *Coda*, October 1973

someone showed me how to really check up on the statements, and that's how I found out that this company was cheating me out of a lot of money. So I just got disgusted because I put all my trust in it, you know, and I stopped. During these five years I had a few students here and there, but mostly I was driving a taxicab here in New York.

To go back some years, how did you actually get into jazz?

I had studied with a private teacher, and naturally I studied classical music. When I graduated from high school, which was an automotive high school, a friend of mine introduced me to a fellow, Steve Pulliam, who was a trombonist. I had gotten a job as an automobile mechanic, and one day I was coming home from work and I happened to run into this fellow who told me that someone wanted to see me. He took me to Steve Pulliam's house, and Steve asked me to play Honeysuckle Rose or any tune I could think of at the piano. As he liked the way I played, I started playing with his band, and that was the band that went out to the New York World's Fair in 1939. They did a contest there for small bands, and it turned out that we won the first prize. So from then on I gave up the job as a mechanic and played with the Steve Pulliam Sextet, playing dance halls mostly. After that I started in the Village, McDougal's was the name of the place, it was on McDougal Street, and I worked there with just a bass player. Later on I got a job with a drummer called Jack Parker, who worked in a few different clubs in New York. Then I joined the Savoy Sultans and I guess you know the rest. From the Savoy Sultans I played with Teddy Walters, and from there I went with Charlie Parker.

Your influences?

My two favorites were Teddy Wilson and Art Tatum.

You also played with other groups besides the Charlie Parker Quintet.

Oh yes, a number of different odd groups. I played with Stan Getz, and I had a few gigs with Sonny Stitt and Gene Ammons off and on. There were so many different names, I can't even think of them all. I played like two weeks with this guy, a month with this guy, three weeks with somebody else. Things like that, which didn't amount to much but was a means of making some money.

Tell me how you met Charlie Parker.

I was working down at the Three Deuces with a guitarist. Charlie Parker came down one night and he said, "Wow, listen to that guy playing." And when the set was over, he asked me would I like to play with his band. He was forming a new band, and as I had heard of Charlie Parker, I naturally said yes. It turned out to be the famous quintet with Tommy Potter, Max Roach, Miles Davis, and myself. Before I met Charlie Parker someone had taken me down to the 78th Street Tap Room to listen to him one night. This was before I joined him so I knew how he could play.

The new music at that time was also developing from the experiments at places like Minton's Playhouse and Clark Monroe's Uptown House. Did you participate in any of these sessions?

Yes, at Minton's Playhouse, with Thelonious Monk, Bud Powell, Walter Bishop, Kenny Drew, myself, and a few other guys. It was a nightclub; they had a bar in front and in the back they had this room where you could buy drinks and sit down and listen to the music. They had a stage back there. I came there pretty often, and you had to be known, so to speak, for coming there before you would be admitted to the back. In other words, they would have to know your face to admit you.

Do you think that the innovations of that time have been fully exploited?

I figure they could be exploited a little further. But there's been a tremendous interruption, as you know of, with this rock and roll thing, which I don't like. Of course, some of the things are put together in good fashion so you can appreciate what is being done. But like you ask me if I think that particular type of music could have been exploited even more, yes, I do think so. However, the interruption took the trend of thought and just stopped it.

The way I see it—and I'm not the only one who feels this way—it seems as if it got to the point where some people who were in power felt as though the black musicians were at the stage where they had a monopoly as far as playing this type of music. So in order to correct this, they said, well, we'll go to the folklore music so we can get our own people into it. So that's how it started, and it wound up into the rock thing. Of course, both black and white musicians are doing the folklore and the rock thing nowadays, but as far as that particular jazz idiom, there were few white musicians who could keep up with the black musicians at that time. Well, there were Al Haig, Gerry Mulligan, Serge Chaloff—I can't name all of them, but there were a few that could keep up with the black musicians. The majority of the white guys, they didn't even know what was going on. They would ask the question, "What are you guys doing?"

Who do you consider to be the most important musicians of that period?

I would say that Charlie Parker was the one who influenced most musicians. Thelonious Monk had his thing. A lot of musicians don't want to admit it, but when Art Tatum did his thing, a lot of things were copied from him but were not admitted being copied. Yes, a lot of things were taken from his records. There was a place on 138th Street between 7th and Lenox Avenues, an after-hours spot where Art Tatum used to appear. He just liked to go up to that place and sit down and play, and they would give him free drinks. A lot of musicians used to go up just to listen to him play, and as I said a lot of things at that particular time were taken from what he played and added to the new music that was coming up. Nobody can take all the credit for the new things, of course, but Charlie Parker, in my opinion, was the first one to come out to play the alto saxophone the way he did. Johnny Hodges played the alto saxophone, but he played it in a completely different way. Today it doesn't seem like anything new is coming out as far as innovation is concerned.

You don't feel that much has happened since that time?

No, since that time, no. And to go back to that period, I liked Thelonious Monk for some of the tunes he wrote, but as far as playing an instrument Charlie Parker—you couldn't take it away—was the most melodic and thoughtful innovator around.

Tell us about your time with the Charlie Parker Quintet.

Well, the band had Max Roach on drums, Tommy Potter on bass, Miles Davis on trumpet, Charlie Parker, and myself. Of course, as the years went by Bird formed different bands and he had different people in it. But his first band is the one I'm speaking about. I liked playing with Charlie Parker, in particular because he was the type of person who would come up with something new all the time. It was a time when everyone was trying to get himself established, so you had to associate with as many musicians as possible so your name would be spoken. Like Minton's Playhouse was a sort of a meeting place for musicians, and by going up there you would meet all the different musicians and they would get a chance to hear each other—which was one way of getting work. About myself, I would say that I was accepted more or less. I could have been accepted better than I was, but on the other hand at that time John Lewis was studying, and from what I understand his parents put the money up for him to study here in New York. My parents didn't have enough money, so I had to pick my things up from here and there. It was a time when you gathered as much knowledge as you could from picking here and picking there, meeting this guy and meeting that guy, and asking questions and listening to the different musicians. A lot of people used to connect me with Bud Powell, but he had his distinctive style and I had mine. He was rated at that time as the boy wonder.

After Charlie Parker you played with Stan Getz, among others. I guess that playing with Getz must have been quite a change from playing with Parker?

Oh, yes, definitely, because Stan Getz had his own way of playing and naturally Charlie Parker had his. The trend of thought was different, completely. But I enjoyed playing with Stan Getz, too, because he can play, there's no denying it, he can really play. I'll have to say that Charlie Parker naturally was more original. Stan Getz can get over the saxophone very well, he was very technical on his horn. But as far as coming out with new passages or new ways of making a run on a chord, running through the changes, you couldn't take it away—Charlie Parker had it. He had so many different ways of attacking a chord that it would make you laugh sometimes. As I said, Stan Getz was very technical in the way he played, but for originality Charlie Parker had it.

Where did he get it all from?

Well, that's a good question. In fact, during many of the intermissions we would take walks around the block and I would talk with him and ask him—"Bird, how did you fall into this way of thinking?" And he would always laugh and say, "Man, I don't know, it's just one of those things." He was a genius and I'm just sorry that he didn't stay here longer. A lot of the things that I heard him play and the way he played them, naturally, I'm trying to get under my fingers. Like the break he took in "A Night in Tunisia," it's a classic. I don't think anyone else will come along to top that—not for a long time.

Charlie Parker influenced a lot of musicians, of course, and not only saxophone players.

Right—trumpet players, clarinet players, piano players. Even Max Roach. Max Roach does things on the drums that are based on things Charlie Parker did.

Were you still in contact with Charlie Parker after you left the band?

Oh, yes, and I still played with him on and off. I went to Detroit to work with Paul Bascomb for a while, and while I was there I got the word that Bird was going to Paris. At the time I got to New York, around two o'clock in the afternoon, I found out that they had left in the morning. He had got the word that I was coming to town, but as he couldn't find me. Al Haig went instead. It was a last-minute thing, you know.

Charlie Parker seemed to prefer you as his pianist, and also you and he were personal friends. Do you think that fact helped making the music better?

Definitely, because you can express yourself better. The closer you are with someone the more intimate you can get, and the more intimate you get the more things you discuss.

You also played in several European countries. It would be interesting to hear your comments as to the attitude of the European audiences compared to the attitude of the audiences in the States.

Well, I found no matter where I went in Europe the audiences were, I would say, ninety percent more interested in what you were doing. In other words, they would be much more attentive, they would be much quieter, they would be listening rather than talking. Of course, some people would be talking, but it would be in a much more subdued way than here in the States. It seems like here everybody wants everybody else to know what they're into, everybody wants to be the top, the big cheese, so to speak, so they talk loud so someone else can hear them. And the smarter they talk and the hipper they talk, their names will get around. That attitude to me is stinko; I don't go for that. That's why I say I go for the attitude they have in Europe a hundred percent more. Because at least they are listening to what you are doing. And another thing I appreciate—if you get on stage and you don't produce or do your best, the audience will let you know. You may have a tomato in your face or a beer can or something thrown at you. Because the audience feels, after all, they feel they are spending their hard-earned money to come and see you. They expect you to do your best. Yes, I appreciate the European audiences much more than the audiences here.

In Europe you made the soundtrack to a French film and also toured with a play, *The Connection.*

Right. The film was *Les liaisons dangereuses.* I wrote the music for that, but I did not like the way the situation turned out. I recorded the music but the company that recorded it ran out of business, and of course the company was Charlie Parker Records.

About *The Connection,* I thought the play was very good, the idea of it. It was a message, but it wasn't trying to say "This is the way it's supposed to be," or lay any morality or anything. You were supposed to form your own opinion on what was going on. In fact, a lot of places we played, the public didn't even know what the play was all about. They thought that some of the actors were acting drunk. In Germany they didn't know what was going on. In Paris, of course, they knew there, and a few places in Sweden they knew also. Anyhow, they liked the music, and everywhere we played we got a good hand. We went to all the different countries in Europe with the play, and I heard a lot of European musicians and appreciated what they were doing. It's just too bad that they can't get the exposure that you get here.

What have you been doing musically in the '60s?

Like I said, I stopped for those five years. I wasn't doing much of anything then, but recently I have been practicing again and trying to get the dexterity back in my fingers. I have been writing some new things, but I'm still leery of where to put them. Of course, I'm connected with BMI, but I think the best thing for me to do now is to form my own music publishing company. That way I'll be sure of collecting the royalties that are due me. On the other hand, when you form your own publishing company, you have to worry about how much exposure you are going to get on records, and when the record company finds out that you have your own company they don't want to give you too much exposure because they don't own the music.

So you plan to form your own publishing company?

Yes. I have written some new things, but now I have to wait on getting the record date so I can have them played. I would say that in another month I will have a complete record date arranged—if I could only get the record date to do it!

What do think could be done in the States to make the situation better for jazz and jazz musicians?

I would say an exchange of musicians. For instance, take five Danish musicians and take five American musicians, and let the Danish musicians come to New York and let the New York musicians go to Denmark for a period of six months. Let the Danish musicians get the exposure that they deserve, and in Denmark let the American musicians get their exposure. That way I figure the public would get a chance to hear what's going on, more or less, in other parts of the world as far as music is concerned.

Also, radio and TV could help by opening up their stations to jazz much more than they do. Only a few stations are featuring jazz on their programs, while most stations are playing rock and roll all day long. And one thing that jazz could stand as long as I can remember is the promoting part of it. Because the public doesn't understand what's going on. They see a guy get up on the stage and they hear him play. But as far as knowing what he is doing, they don't know. It could be explained to them very easily so they could understand much more of what the musician is doing and why he's doing it. The disc jockeys could very easily take the time to explain about the music, and they could do it in a way that wouldn't take up too much time. If they're playing a record by Sonny Stitt, they could say, for instance, "And now, ladies and gentlemen, this is Sonny Stitt and he is playing such and such a tune. And listen for this and the way he does this, and the reason why he does this is because blah–blah–blah. . . . And he has been doing this such and such a time before, and now go and listen for yourself." And when the record is over, explain a little further and then let it go. And I don't feel that is too much. The disc jockeys could do a lot by saying different things to get the people interested. As to colleges and schools, they should do more to explain what jazz is about. It is beginning to get better at schools, but it is too slow, much too slow.

Could musicians themselves do something to help each other?

Of course. They could help each other in numerous ways. If one guy is working at a good club, he could talk to the owner, recommend certain artists, and get the owner interested in booking some of these musicians.

It seems like some musicians never get a chance to record, while others are recording all the time.

Right. I find that there's a game of politics going on. What I mean by that is that some musicians have found that the musicians that have a name and get the record dates. . . . When they do see them, they associate with them, buy them drinks, talk with them, light their cigarettes, and all that. They cater to these musicians, and those are the ones who wind up getting the record dates with these particular top stars. I find that even down by the union, guys come down and they find the people who have the *in*, so to speak, as far as the clubs are concerned. And it's the same thing all over again. They are Uncle Toms to them, but they wind up with the jobs. Well, I suppose everybody likes to be catered to.

The other night you told me that you were still composing and tonight you said the same thing, so you feel you are still developing as an artist?

Definitely, yes. I feel as though new ideas are coming to me and my fingers are beginning to loosen up to the point I would like them to. But I'm still not to the point where I'm satisfied—far from it. But I feel that one day I'll get there since I've got the determination to get there. I feel as though I'll do it.

Which records do you consider your best?

There was one record I did with Charlie Parker Records. It was the music of the picture *Les liaisons dangereuses*. I think that was a good date. And also a record I did with Blue Note, *Flight to Jordan*. But those were my beginning years, and now if I make a record date I will make sure, much more sure, that everything is done the way it's supposed to be done and that the musicians will be the right musicians. Like on that record date I did with Blue Note, I had a trumpet player, Dizzy Reece, and I shouldn't have given him the date. I should have given it to someone else because he didn't jell with Stanley Turrentine, the saxophone player. It was a wrong combination, and the record date didn't come out the way it should have.

Have you already thought of some musicians you would like to use on a future date?

Oh yeah, there's a number of them around. So many that I hate even to start naming names. If I get the date, as I said, that will be ready the next time.

When I asked about the records you made, I was also thinking of the things you did with Charlie Parker.

Well, I'm satisfied with some of them, not all of them. Some of them I wish I could have done over, and that is also true with some of the things I did with Stan Getz.

You had a specialty with Charlie Parker: the short, lyrical introductions on the ballads.

Yes, everybody seemed to like my introductions. I just got a letter from another guy from Paris, Henri Renaud, and he was telling me that he hadn't seen me in a long time and that he always remembered my introductions on the dates I did with Charlie Parker. And it makes me feel good that people still remember. Like you wrote saying the same thing. About the introductions, I just felt these things and they came out that way. Even sometimes now I'll sit down and play a thing like "Embraceable You" and I'll make the introduction, and as soon as I go into the introduction some people in the audience will say, "Oh, yeah." They will know it right away and that's funny, and naturally I have to appreciate something like that.

Do you have any comments on the scene today?

I would like to see more of the melodic type of music come back. In other words, when Charlie Parker improvised on any tune he was always melodic, he was always telling a pretty story. I would like to see more of that come back rather than this freedom thing they're doing. That type of playing, I can't make it. They say that these guys know what they're doing and maybe they do. But to the ear, to the ordinary ear. . . . I mean, I always keep the ordinary public in mind; I keep saying, well, here's a guy who doesn't know anything about music. He knows what he likes, however, and if something is played and it sounds pretty to him, he will appreciate it. But if something is done and he can't understand and it is harsh at the same time, he's gonna turn his ears off. He's gonna turn the station off to get something that pleases him. So I would like to see much more of the melodic type of playing come back rather soon.

Do you listen to much of the new music being played today?

I listen to it. Every now and then I go to a concert or to a club, but I have my own problems to contend with. I don't feel I get out as much as I could, but I also have to be working as much as possible. Today is the last day of the Newport Jazz Festival and I didn't make any of the concerts because I was working at the Cellar. Maybe next year everything will go right and maybe I'll be invited to play. I'll try to form my own thing.

What kind of group would you prefer to lead?

I would like to have a quintet because that way I could write some music for it. With a trio I could have some arrangements to play—myself, the drummer, and the bass player—and we could hit things together. But to get a bigger sound, I would like to start with a quintet—like a trombone and baritone, or a tenor and a trumpet, or alto and trumpet, something like that.

Several of the musicians you have talked about are still playing. Miles Davis and Max Roach, for example.

Yes, and Tommy Potter is making a few gigs here and there. He doesn't come on the scene as much as he should, and I understand that he has been working in a hospital. As you say, Max has his group and Miles is doing his thing.

Why is it that some musicians make it while others . . .

It's a matter of business, maneuver so to speak. From what I understand, when Miles formed his new group, the first thing he did was to contact a lawyer, a young lawyer who was interested in handling musicians. This particular guy Miles was up with helped him tremendously, so when Miles came up with an idea of . . . whatever it might be, he would say to his lawyer, "Hey, look, man, this guy is giving me a hard time. I'm supposed to be here four weeks but I'm going to be here two weeks and then quit because I don't dig what's going on. What kind of trouble can I get into if I do this?" And the lawyer would straighten him out. These kinds of things. Of course, it came to the point where Miles made some money and he took it and invested it in blue-chip stock. In other words, every time they turn the lights on in New Jersey, Miles is collecting some money. That makes him independent, and once you're independent you can demand this and you can demand that. But of course, at the same time he's gotten together with Gil Evans—and when he comes upon any ideas musically, he gets together with Gil Evans and he tells Gil to write such and such and Gil arranges the music the way Miles wants it.

As for myself, I stuck to what I wanted to do more or less. From what I understand a lot of people like what I'm doing, and a lot of others feel I could be much more close to what Bud Powell was doing. However, I want to be an individualist. I feel I've got my thing to say, and let me say it my way like Bud said it his way.

Do you read reviews and do you think you learn anything from it?

Definitely, because each individual thinks his own way and they can give you ideas. Some guy may say something that may strike you in a certain way and you might correct. I like to be criticized; I like to read what they say because there are so many individuals, and each one has his own thoughts. One guy may say that you're tops and another guy would say that you stink. And behind this guy saying that you stink, he might make you think about something that you weren't thinking about. Which may make you better. That's the way I look at it.

Jackie McLean

$\mathcal{H}$aving started on alto saxophone at fifteen, Jackie McLean (1932–2006) soon be-friended Bud Powell, Kenny Drew, and Sonny Rollins and did his debut recording with Miles Davis in 1951. His sharp, biting sound was immediately recognizable and he often played with Davis, Art Blakey, and Charles Mingus during the '50s. From 1959, he led his own groups and recorded extensively for Blue Note, taking his inspiration from Charlie Parker one step further, and one of his LPs featured Ornette Coleman as a side-man. He spent time in Europe during the early '70s, after which education and teaching took more of his time, particularly so after he became head of the Jazz Department at Hartford University. Since the mid-'80s he has again been very active as a player, often coleading groups with his son, tenor player Rene M. (b. 1946).

Right now I'm living in Hartford, teaching at the university. The way I'm situated now is that I more or less teach from September until May, and then I try to use that period between May and September to play as much as I can. I have purposely been staying out of the nightclubs, and until I find the right situation again in New York I won't be playing there. Slugs was the place that I sort of started playing in. That club went from nothing to a major jazz club, and then it was finished with the death of Lee Morgan. The vibrations surrounding the nightclub scene today just turn me off. I enjoy playing for the people; I enjoy the setting. I know I contradict myself every time I try to explain it, but I have so many other feelings about music that I didn't have before that it sort of puts a bad taste in my mouth when I play and I don't see children there and I don't see it becoming an educational situation—just playing for people drinking. It's strange, at the Montmartre here in Copenhagen there's a feeling I get that people are there and that their reason for being there is to listen to the music. And it just happens that there are some beers and things that they take along with it. In some clubs in the States, I get the feeling that people come there to drink, and they accompany their drinking with the major jazz artists.

Previously published in *Coda*, January 1974

In Hartford, I'm developing a cultural program for the community people, and that's where I'm going to be playing. That's where I'll be trying to bring major jazz artists to play for the people. We have already developed our program in Hartford, and we have received some help from the state of Connecticut. Our program is called the Artists Collective, and I'll explain that to you.

We are five artist that have come together to form this Artists Collective and bring culture to the area. First of all, in dance we have a young lady who is very talented, by the name of Cheryl Smith. She was born and raised in Hartford and has been doing things in dance there for years. Ionis Martin is the person doing visual arts, and my wife, Dollie, was once affiliated with a Negro ensemble company that is very famous today. She was a part of their workshop and has learned a lot about theater, and so she came to help me working in drama. Also, we brought up a gentleman, Roger Furman, using him as our artist-in-residence. We did his play *The Long Black Block*. Barbara Hudson is our executive director. In my music department, I have a young man who I think is going to make an influence on the music business. His name is Billy Gault, and he plays every instrument and he writes. He's a fantastic piano player, that's his main instrument, and he and I wrote the music for Furman's play. That's the kind of things we're trying to do. At the university, my title is director of Afro-American studies. Our aim is to be a cultural program.

Does this program also include a political involvement?

Well, it's hard not to become politically involved when you work within the state and the community. We try not to be politically involved; we say that we are only concerned with the art and concerned with the passing of the culture from the artist to the person in the community. There always comes a time when you need political figures to help you continue your program, but we try to avoid as much politics as possible.

How was the reaction from the audience to *The Long Black Block*?

It's quite a provocative play, and people reacted in many ways. Some were shocked; others were overwhelmed and shocked but enjoyed it anyway. The play has funny moments and it has tragic moments. It's very hard to describe. You'll have to see it yourself to really understand it. Actually, we're planning to try to set up some kind of package and maybe come this way with our cultural program to present jazz and drama. Years back, I was involved with another play, *The Connection*, and that's where I started getting interested in that kind of thing.

You made an album over here last summer, but apart from that you haven't been recording at all for several years.

At one time recording was my only livelihood. Because they had the cabaret card situation, I was not able to work in New York. As my recording contracts were never what they should have been, I decided in 1967 that I wouldn't sign again unless I received ample money. As I never did, I decided to record only when I wanted to record. When I recorded this recent album for Nils Winther's SteepleChase label, I did it also because Nils wanted me to do it very much and because he had a desire to make a good record. I decided I would sacrifice and help him. I may do another album for Nils, and I'm doing the Alto Saxophone Summit album here in Copenhagen shortly.

Many American musicians have made Europe their home. The other day I talked to a young American drummer, Howard King, who told me he would never want to leave New York.

Howard is a young man who has worked with my son and has worked with me, and I feel at this point in Howard's career he should be in New York. When you mature to Dexter Gordon's age, you sort of take your inspiration with you. That goes for people like Johnny Griffin and others, who have come to Europe. Myself, I find inspiration from the Hartford area, where I'm living. I think we play different in different places.

Do you see any differences between the new and the older generations of musicians? I am not only talking about the music, but also of the entire attitude of the musicians.

Yes. Like I said, I don't look to the older musicians for inspiration. I look to the young people. They are more concerned about where the music is being played and the whole playing situation. When I was coming up society had made it so that most musicians were destroying themselves, drinking, using drugs. . . . And I think that the young musicians have challenged these things; they have been able to refuse these things. Also, they are not so concerned with the competitive aspect. When I was coming up, you had to be the king of the tenor saxophone, etc. The young musicians now are helping each other much more. They realize that each musician has something to say of his own, and they are not competing the same way as before. They may compete to play better, but it's not that gladiator situation; it's more of a group feeling. I like that very much, and as I said I look to the young musicians for inspiration, and I've had the pleasure of helping some of these young people.

A lot of musicians disappear or just can't make it. Could anything be done to help this?

I think that one of the most important things and one of the most beautiful things that could happen would be a final recognition of this music, the Afro-American music, in the educational system—not only in the United States but throughout the world. I know that's a pretty big step, but I think it's about time that the step was taken. It's obvious that Afro-American music is here, and I don't think there's a corner of this globe where you can go today and not find elements of the Afro-American input in music. We learn about classical music in school. I know I certainly did, and I think if we really began to study and teach the young children about the many, many areas of Afro-American music, they would begin to learn about some musicians who now are obsolete because there isn't any audience for the music.

I'm here in Copenhagen playing at the Montmartre and it's a fine audience, but when I talk to people here in Denmark I find out that it's just a very few people who are really turning out to hear the music. As far as what could be done, I think besides having the music become part of the curriculum in the education in the early learning centers throughout the world, I think that people who do know about some of the obsolete musicians or some of the guys who have disappeared from the scene, they could write in and ask, "Where is Tommy Potter?" or "Where is Duke Jordan?" It would take hours to think about all of them and relate their names to you. Like John Jenkins, a very fine alto saxophone player, and there's the vice president, Paul Quinichette. What happened to Paul Quinichette? There are so many, and these musicians gave me a lot of pleasure in my life. It's so beautiful to hear Dexter Gordon and Gene Ammons, but a lot of the musicians who have done so much to bring happiness to so many of us are off the scene. And I imagine that they feel that no one cares because no one writes in. No one writes in to the magazines, and no one tries to form small organizations like you have tried to do over here in Denmark in order to collect some money and invite a couple of musicians over here every year.

You talked about the young musicians and the jazz tradition and the need of explaining to the young people about the great jazz artists . . .

There are a lot of fine young musicians around and I don't know half of them now. I had the pleasure of going down to hear McCoy Tyner's quartet the other night. I have played a lot with Juney Booth, the bass player, and Al Muzon, the drummer, in the past, but the tenor player was a brand-new face on the scene, Azar Lawrence. He's a fantastic young man, and I must say that hearing him this week was very inspiring to me. I get inspiration from many of the young musicians, like my son, Rene McLean, James Benjamin, Billy Gault, and now Azar. There are so many young ones who are around the New York City area, but also there are many in the outlying areas. I know there's a young alto player in San Francisco named Norman Williams, who really sounds beautiful.

I think it's important for the young musicians to organize and try to get grants from the government to set up smaller music centers that can function within the inner city by having jazz workshops and history courses. I also would suggest that the young musicians do not make the mistakes I did, waiting so many years to investigate all Afro-American music. I naturally knew about Louis Armstrong and had heard of King Oliver and Jelly Roll Morton, but when I finally had the opportunity to teach in a university, it gave me the incentive to really research and to check out the history. I always wish I had started to do this reading much earlier in my life because there's a wealth of information there—for example, about the black piano players, like Scott Joplin in the 1880s and 1890s. These piano players were playing ragtime music, and if the young musicians are going to absorb it, there should be small history classes and demonstration workshops to really get young kids interested in this fine music.

· 6 ·

Mary Lou Williams

Mary Lou Williams (1910–1981) played piano with vaudeville shows starting in her teens and was pianist and arranger with Andy Kirk's orchestra before she was twenty. After leaving Kirk in 1942, she led her own small bands and wrote scores for Benny Goodman, Duke Ellington, and Dizzy Gillespie's big band, among others. For some years in the '50s she retired from music but she remained active throughout the '60s and '70s playing with her own groups, composing sacred works, and teaching. Never one to seek the limelight, she often encouraged and supported younger players, who also inspired her own playing, and several of the young beboppers considered her their mentor. She was often involved in charity work, and her Christian faith influenced several of her compositions: cantatas and masses. Her playing and knowledge encompassed all kinds of jazz, and her openness and lack of prejudice was legendary.

My favorite piano players were Jelly Roll Morton, Earl Hines, Fats Waller, and James P. Johnson. Those are the people I liked from that era. I guess the reason I always stayed ahead of everything, and why I always was able to play different styles, was because I experienced quite a lot in music.

These pianists you mention were people who played in cities and were making records. Were there any local piano players you listened to? In a way, Art Tatum was a local pianist in the '20s, wasn't he?

Yes, but I hadn't met Art Tatum; no one had heard about Art Tatum then. You see, the only pianists I heard on records were Jelly Roll Morton and Earl Hines. Hines was from my hometown, Pittsburgh, and we used to go to the afternoon dances to hear him. I think I met Tatum in the '30s, the early '30s, even before he left Toledo. At that time I was traveling with Andy Kirk's band and we had a layoff in Toledo, Ohio, and that's when I first met him.

    I met Pete Johnson in Kansas City around 1930 when they had those terrific sessions. We worked from nine to twelve, and at that time Pete Johnson,

Previously published in *Coda*, July 1974

Hot Lips Page, and all of them would be playing, for instance, *Sweet Georgia Brown*. I would go home and change my uniform—it was in the summer—take a bath, and change, and when I got back they were still playing *Sweet Georgia Brown*. There were about fifteen musicians and it sounded like a big arrangement, and we would sit there and jam all night. It was such a beautiful thing to be in Kansas City. All the musicians were so wonderful, and as it was during the Depression people didn't have much money. We would go out, everybody would share, stay out late, and jam. It was such a beautiful era. I think Kansas City is the most important era in the music. I remember Charlie Parker wearing knee pants. He was going to high school, and he and Andy Kirk's wife, Mary, were in a little nightclub playing together. Everybody said, "That horn sounds funny playing with her." He was playing the same style as he did later on—way out—and we listened to them and just laughed. In Kansas City they had at least five or six bands and two of them were high school boys, and Charlie Parker would come and swing everybody out. The union would give a dance to raise money and Charlie Parker was in this band.

You are one of the first people who have mentioned meeting and hearing Thelonious Monk.

I don't know if I was the first, but I met him in 1930 or 1931. He was traveling with a medicine or carnival show, some kind of show. He decided to stay in Kansas City, and we became friends and were very close. He was the same kind of person then—he never talked. But I think it's his way, and when he does open his mouth it's important what he says.

You know when I was in the band, they wouldn't allow me to talk. It was, "Put everything into your music" and "keep your mouth shut." I couldn't even talk to anybody for years. All they wanted was to do music, think music, sleep music.

There was a pause in your musical career in the 50s . . .

Everybody asks me why I stopped. I don't even know why; I just stopped. I was in England and they gave me a birthday party. But what happened was that I just locked my bag and went to Paris and stayed there for about eleven months. I don't know why I stopped, but I began praying, leaving all my clothes and things in England. Nothing happened. I guess I was just sick of it all for a while. In Paris, a French drummer who plays with all the American musicians took me out to his grandmother's house, where I stayed.

Religion is a part of every jazz musician. God has quite a bit to do with jazz. You know the black Americans have been very badly mistreated in America, but God gave us jazz, he gave this art, the greatest art in the world, and he gave it to everybody. And it's love because God is the God of love, and there's no color barrier. Everybody plays it. Because Zoot Sims has a soul like nobody has. This music is not for one person to play and call himself or herself the king or queen of jazz. This music was put on earth to help people, and it's the greatest art and it will never be destroyed. Lately, some musicians have been looking for false stars. If they look around themselves and just do their work, that's God, but they're looking for something else.

Were you always a Catholic?

I'll tell you what happened. I'm a guinea pig and anything I tell you is more or less true. I don't listen to what people tell me, and Andy Kirk used to give me hell about that. You tell me something, and I'll go out and try it. Of course, that doesn't go for stuff like heroin, but I have to see things.

When I began praying and everything, people said that everything was going to be so bad in the '60s and '70s. When I began praying that way, the Catholic church was the only church that was open and peaceful. A lot of other musicians began preaching and began doing things like that because they felt things the way I did. So I began going to the church, and that's how I became a Catholic. I find it is a true religion. People may have their own religion and whatnot, but that's really a great way of reaching love, that church, the Catholic church. I don't want to push it on anybody, but that's what I discovered. It teaches you how to live and it teaches you how to love your neighbor, and if you have any rocks or anything they're gone. And something else about them. I can drink as long as I don't drink up all the money that I'm going to use for my rent; they don't bar you from a lot of things that other religions do. Like you shouldn't do this and you shouldn't do that, and fast and starve and all that. You fast if you want to, if the spirit tells you to fast. That's your faith. You can drink, you can gamble, you can do anything you want to. But it's sin when you gamble for the money you should use for your family, for your household. I like the liturgy, I like the way they teach, and I think it's difficult to get to it. If you're selfish, you probably would never become a Catholic. Everybody will put the thing down, but I found out what it was all about, so this is where I'll stay. And I'm lucky because I think there's a spirit in all these things. I go down and meditate in that church, and I hear some crazy arrangements. They come so fast I can't write them.

Let's move to another subject. In a way, jazz is an extremely male kind of music, you might say. Except for singers, perhaps all the great jazz artists have been men. How have you felt about that?

Jazz is a male kind of music, right, but let me tell you the truth about it. Since I was three or four years old, men have had me on their lap. Sometimes we all make mistakes, men and women, but they come to me. . . . And Monk said once to his wife, "There's only one woman that I'll listen to and that's Mary Lou Williams. The others around are all silly and they don't have anything to say." And Bud Powell was the same way. You see, I'm not comfortable around women. If you put me with a hundred men, I can just sit there and go to sleep. Now, when I was in grade school they would come to Pittsburgh and take me out on the gigs. Men have been helping me all my life.

When I began playing, my mother was so surprised. She played organ, and one day when she was pumping the organ I began to pick up melodies, and I was nothing but a baby. I must have been twelve or thirteen years old when I met Fats Waller. He was in the Cotton Club with someone who said, "See that little girl sitting there. She can play everything you wrote today." I was brought up to Fats Waller, and I played one thing he had just finished composing. Fats Waller was the most terrific composer in the world. You see, men picked me up and taught me everything. I was walking on the roughest streets in Pittsburgh when I was going to school. I was walking everywhere and nobody would ever bother me. I would be jamming with Chu Berry, among others.

I have starved. I have gone two or three months without eating as the situation at home wasn't too good. So if somebody comes up to me to complain or something, I'll say, "Have you starved ten years with the band?" Two or three of them died, but I kept on because I love music. You learn something from starving and from your lack of money. That's something I discovered, that's something else the liturgy taught me. The hard work. I used to sit at the piano when I was ten years old, and when I wasn't in school I would sit there from 8 o'clock in the morning until 10 at night and nobody gave me food or water or anything.

You have been involved in social work helping sick musicians . . .

Yes, I had a foundation. However, I had to drop it because I went back to music and playing again. It seems that if I start something everybody else will be doing the same. A few years ago nothing was happening, no jazz at all. But Dizzy Gillespie wouldn't let me rest; Dizzy gave me the guts. He gave me a mink stole, but I didn't want any mink. He gave me a watch that I just lost. It cost $400. He tried to keep me on—all the musicians did. They had the feeling that if I started playing, the whole thing would start rolling again. We went to California, and before that Father O'Connor was trying to get me come out. Sometimes you're not used to big success; you're used to helping others.

Doesn't a female musician face some obstacles that male musicians don't? Won't she always be met with prejudices?

When I play, you can't tell that a man isn't playing. Do you know any other woman who has the force of a man about their playing? I play like a man, and that's why I got my reputation. When I'm really blowing, I play exactly like a man. You won't miss it—I know that. Other women may be playing more, but they don't have that mannish thing. That's something developed by me being around men. And I think like men. You see, there's a lot of male pianists that sound like women. They feel that way and they're not pushing as much as me. Also, many women make excuses, but I don't make excuses because I was trained the rough way. When we were here in New York at a jam session with Louis Armstrong and Fats Waller and all those great people, I was brought in to play, and somebody said they would punch me in my mouth if I didn't play. I was brought up like a man—I mean, they would knock me off the piano. I made an introduction once, and—"Don't make that anymore, that doesn't sound good!" And bang!

Benny Carter, Fats Waller. . . . I've been on jam sessions with big-time names since I was twelve years old or younger, and I played with Duke Ellington's band. I remember George Lee going to rehearsals with a gun hidden under a newspaper. The musicians have it easy now; I didn't have it easy at all. The '30s saw the last of the world-trained musicians, and out of that came Charlie Parker and Dizzy. They knew what they were doing because they were trained. There's a lot of talking to do after you learn to play your instrument, and you have to listen to everything any older person tells you about your instrument. When I was working with Andy Kirk and began writing music, Andy Kirk would sit with me from 11 o'clock in the morning till 12 at night writing. So I was watching and learning. I made arrangements, but they were head arrangements. The first tunes I did around 1929 for Brunswick—"Froggy Bottom" and all that—were my arrangements, but Andy Kirk would write them down. And so I learned to arrange myself by watching him. The Andy Kirk band had great readers; they could play anything.

When did you start writing for other bands? Was that when you left Andy Kirk?

No, no. I started writing for all the bands. John Hammond asked me to write something for Benny Goodman when Goodman was really at his peak, and I did "Roll 'Em." We wouldn't play a boogie—the band wouldn't because that had a bad thing in back of it. People would consider it a Negro thing when it was played, and there are things to be played in jazz other than boogie. Most black people, even during that era, didn't like the boogie because it was a bad thing. It means you're a nigger, and it means let's go out and have a ball with the girls. After I did the arrangements for Benny Goodman. . . . You know, I got an awful lot of money for that arrangement because it was something the musicians wanted to play. I experimented a lot. As we only had three saxophones, I would put a trumpet in a muted hat for four saxophones. Also I used to mute a trombone to play with the saxophones to get a sound. That's how I started arranging, and when I had to do something heavy I just went to a friend or I would call the union. There was a girl down there who was terrific. I knew a guy who taught me all the sounds of John Coltrane. This was in the '40s and the guy's name was Milton Orent, and he knew so much that he couldn't play. He was going to learn jazz and then I learned from him, writing and sounds and things. When Sarah Vaughan and people would come up, Milton would sit at the piano and play some way-out changes. Miles Davis used to come up, too, and he didn't like it. Milton played way-out sounds like Coltrane, and that was when I was in Café Society. I have some of the music here now. Milton was very good.

Do you feel that the jazz audience has changed?

No, I don't feel the audience has changed as much as the musicians, who all want to be greater than the other. It's like it's so much ego now. Before there was so much more happiness in it. A man is only great if he can play everything. Now they just want to play one style. However, they won't stay around me because they're afraid of my ears. I can hear what they play. So it's pretty bad when they talk about other people and what they are not doing. I think that's pretty bad, and we have quite a bit of that now. I think that if you can practically do everything that's happening out there, you're like James Moody—you're nice. Like Dizzy—he's nice. Dizzy doesn't only help me, he helps a lot of poor people. He gets kids to school; he teaches them in his basement. He's a great musician and they should all be like that.

But it does happen that great musicians are not, perhaps, sympathetic people.

Because they have something missing in their talent. Jazz can tell you how evil a person is, but the musicians don't know that. If a musician is up there playing pretty with a sound and everything, you can feel how he is from what he's playing.

Would you say, for instance, that Charlie Parker was always such a nice person?

Yes, he was. Charlie Parker destroyed himself. I knew Charlie, he and Monk and Bud Powell—we were all friends. They used to come up here for inspiration. Charlie Parker was nice, but he might not have been able to teach any-body because he was hung up. Miles was terrific then, not like he is now. When I saw him in England, he would try to be nice and everything, but something very bad happened to him when Birdland was opened. Miles used to stand outside and he was beaten by the police, and since that time he has been kind of off. And Babs Gonzales used to be a nice guy, but some people are weak and they cannot take suffering. It changes them and makes them evil.

You know what evil is? It's what Miles just did when he made some state-ments to the press about the Newport Jazz Festival and some of the musicians performing there. I didn't read it, but someone told me. Evil is to get a man out of work, to say bad things about him to get him out of work. If you and I know someone, well, we could talk about him, but to say it in the paper like that—that's very bad. Selfishness and bitterness will make you evil. If I take all the money myself and don't give you anything when you come to my door, or if I'm being jealous of someone. . . . Those are the things that make you evil. You know, I saw Miles in England and he just grabbed and hugged me and kissed me, but I was afraid of him. I thought that if he would assault me, I would go and assault him. I hear what he's playing; he's playing the same style practically he has always played. But now he's got the modern thing in back of him, the guys who make the noise. Like Stan Getz—it's the same thing. He has a group with all that stuff, but Stan Getz still plays pretty. Listen to his tone, listen to his chord changes and you'll hear it. So Miles Davis really has no reason to say anything about Dizzy Gillespie and Sarah Vaughan.

I know that Miles and Dizzy are great friends, and the thing about it is that Miles is playing Dizzy's style. Every trumpet player in the world is play-ing Dizzy. And you know, when Dizzy is playing the slow thing, he's playing Harold Baker. Harold Baker was terrific when he played a slow tune and Miles always said, I heard him say, "Oh, if I could play as high as Dizzy and as sweet as Harold Baker." So he had no reason to say what he said. He's got to be out of his mind because he says all the time that the black Americans are so very badly treated . . .

Like I said, they need a school of love and you should be there ten years before you graduated. That's right because the world, I don't know how it is in Europe, but the United States is pretty bad. It's best always to be nice to people because in the end you get it back. But this is a funny era, and I will be happy when it's over.

· 7 ·

Howard King

Howard King (b. 1955) started listening to jazz when he was ten, and while in junior high school he played drums with the school band. Later he attended the Jazzmobile workshop and listened to and was inspired by drummers such as Art Blakey, Max Roach, and Jack DeJohnette. Also, Miles Davis had a great influence on his playing. He worked with the saxophonist Rene McLean and later with another sax player, Gary Bartz, with whom he also played in Europe in the '70s. King has recorded with organist Larry Young and with Gary Bartz's NTU group.

I started listening to jazz when I was about ten. We had a friend who lived upstairs—he was one of my brother's friends—and he was always listening to jazz. I used to go upstairs sometimes with my brother, and we would listen to tapes. My uncle plays piano, and he was involved with a group in the States called Jazz Interactions for a while. That uncle was an influence to people like Jimmy Smith and that type of thing. The friend would also put on Miles Davis and John Coltrane and someone like that. I really couldn't understand their music at that time, and I didn't like it as I didn't know what was really happening. It took quite a while till I began to stretch out a little more and began to listen to people like Art Blakey, Freddie Hubbard, and Lee Morgan. To understand and appreciate Coltrane, it took some time, and I didn't until 1971, about two years ago. I wish I could have heard him in person. When I was younger, as I said, I preferred to listen to people like Jimmy Smith. I could hear what they were doing a little more. You know, if I couldn't sing what they were playing or just be able to see how it was going, then I didn't understand. As far as instruments, I've always liked the trumpet. Earlier I liked the organ and the vibraphone, but when I began to listen to Blakey I began to appreciate all the different instruments.

When did you start playing yourself?

I started when I was about twelve, in 1968, in the junior high school band. I remember I went down every day and asked if I could be in the band so I

Previously published in *Coda*, November 1974

could play. The first year I was in junior high school I didn't play, but the latter part of the second year I played with the band. The first two years I was playing drums. I was interested, but not really interested. I was just playing because everybody else was playing an instrument in school. After that I started going to a workshop called Jazzmobile. Al "Tootie" Heath, Max Roach, and different drummers used to come down and instruct classes there. I would be playing there with the band, but then somebody else would take over. After a while I would get kind of angry at that, so I went home and practiced and listened. I played baritone horn in school and that's the only instrument I could say I played other than drums. I would like to learn to play piano and bass.

Which drummers did you listen to when you took up music more seriously?

Well, as I said I was listening before I began to play. Speaking of drummers, I listened to Art Blakey, Max Roach, Tony Williams, Roy Haynes, and a lot of younger cats who are starting to be recognized now—Lenny White, Jack DeJohnette, people like them. Even before I started myself, when I was only listening, I used to sing different drum solos. You can almost say that I knew more or less where I was going. Also, Miles Davis had a great influence on my playing. The way he spaced, not playing continuously—I try to develop that playing on the drums. Playing things backwards, forwards, leave stuff out . . . things like that.

The term *loud* is used very often when the playing of Lenny White, Jack DeJohnette, Tony Williams, and yourself is being discussed. You play very loud.

It depends on where your level is. Since I came to Europe, I've noticed that the Europeans eat light, they speak softly, their whole way of living is very casual. And therefore I think maybe they would like to listen to something more subdued. But sometimes you're angry and you play loud, and sometimes you feel different and you play soft. I don't think the people you mentioned play loud all the time, not at all, and I think that when they do play loud there's a reason. I recall one time recently in Chicago a newswriter—he knew nothing about nothing—he wrote that my loud cymbal work would be more suited for a rock band, something like Humble Pie or Jeff Beck. It doesn't really make any difference, but that was the first time I ever read something like that and I got kind of upset about it. So I called Max Roach and told him about it. He told me that way back, even before I was born, they wrote that he couldn't keep time and that Dizzy Gillespie played like he had marbles in his mouth and that Bud Powell played like he only had one hand, etc. So that's the way writers are anyway, most writers.

You talked about taking up other instruments. Do you plan to continue as a drummer or do you have other plans?

In September 1974 I'm going to the University of Massachusetts to take up arranging and composition, which Max told me about. He teaches up there and he told me that he would like to see me arrange for a big band. I have always been thinking of that, like I feel I kind of have a certain knack for arranging music, which I enjoy doing. And then with a big band, your drummers can bash and everything and it doesn't sound loud. I like watching big band drummers. I also want to master music education so I could teach later on. Up in Norway, I talked with Gerald Wilson about that. He's a good example of a big band arranger. I would like to do something along his line and Thad Jones and people like that.

The drummer's role has changed a lot since the time when he was merely a timekeeper.

Yeah, at one time it was more playing fours and a bass drum, mainly keeping the time and catching whatever accent there was but not really playing a lot. But like all the other instruments, the drums have been developed. I think what's happening now is that the drummer kind of keeps his own time. I mean, he's not keeping the time just monotonously. The way all the players are playing now—and this is one of the things Miles had a lot to do with—it's not continuously playing through a chorus. It's spacing and stuff like that. I find that when I'm playing with somebody who plays a lot of notes, there's little I can do other than just keeping time. But somebody like Gary Bartz and Miles and Coltrane and people like that give you much more of a chance to stretch out and this is fun. So a lot has changed.

Which group did you start playing with?

When I really started with the Jazzmobile, I played with a lot of different cats and the band was like a big band. From that, we got together in small groups, and the first person I started really working with was Jackie's son, Rene McLean. Working with him helped me tremendously because most of the time I used to practice, and when I started working with him it gave me a chance to start with other people. In 1972, on April 15 up in Buffalo, I started with Gary Bartz. You see, I did a gig down in Baltimore with Rene, and Gary was there, too. He told me that he was going to call me and he got my number. Gary told me I was going to make a gig in Camden, which I didn't make, though, but he called me and I've been with him ever since.

Since I started working with Gary Bartz, there are numerous things I've learned. Basically what I have learned from Bartz is how to relax and choose, to play and swing. He told me a great deal about playing, and from working with him and different types of people I've learned how to play. Once you have certain things under your belt, you can kind of see what is happening and go for yourself. One of the first things I did with Gary was in Buffalo—we did a concert and then we played in a club. After the first night I went over to him at the bar, and he said to me, "Say, you got the whole week. Are you trying to play all your stuff in one set? Just kind of relax, take it easy." I tried to keep that in mind. The drums are a type of instrument that may cancel everything out. I think you can kind of overshadow the whole thing without knowing it, without being aware of it. The drummer has to be very sensitive in the group because he can kind of control what's coming out. It's important to always keep your ears open and listen to the other members. If you play what you think is appropriate, I think that's all you can do. Everybody else in the group sees where you come in. Some people might hear a whole lot of drums; some people won't.

Could you name some of the other bands today you like to listen to?

Well, I like Miles and Joe Henderson; I like Sonny Rollins' new group and McCoy Tyner. I haven't listened that much to Chick Corea's new band. It's a different kind of music, but I like it. I used to go out and listen a lot, but I haven't had too much time this last year because it was my last year in school. I just tried to relax and do what I wanted to do. And I don't want to go to clubs . . . they stink, they're full of smoke, people are drinking. The only reason I'm in the club is because I'm playing. When I first started playing, the only place for me to go was there—that's where the music is to be played, which is a drag.

Would you like to have the music out of the clubs?

Yes, I mean it's not doing what it should be doing because it's performed in places like that, where people my age can't go because of the alcohol. There's a place called The East in New York, which is a place that doesn't serve alcohol. You can bring your family and listen to music. It's a much more pleasant atmosphere, and I like that. In the normal clubs it's not a healthy kind of atmosphere. Consider classical music, you know, by Stravinsky and all them being performed in places with people sitting around talking and smoking and drinking. Classical music is performed in big halls, where everybody's attention is on the music. I like concerts much more.

Some musicians say that if you are lucky enough to play in a good club, the atmosphere there may be more intimate and make you play better.

Yes, you feel closer to the people, but I feel intimate when I play at The East and there's not a lot of excess talking and alcohol drinking and smoking. When

I come out of a club and go home, my hair smells like the smoke. I mean, you should be able to perform in places with an intimate atmosphere and without alcohol and smoke.

Do you like traveling around as a musician?

Yeah, I do. I never got the chance to travel that much before. I like to go to different places and I never thought I was going to come over here. When I was in school and was learning the language—I don't know how I got through it—my teachers used to say, "You should study the language so later on when you go out. . . ." And I would answer, "I'm not going to other countries; I wanna stay here." And now I'm over here and wish I knew some of the language. You know, reading my history books about Europe was like I never wanted to come here anyway. The way they made it seem, so slow and backwards, and the governments, and the behavior—like locked up, caged up, and anything else. But I enjoy being here, though I don't think I could live here. You ever heard the expression "get down"? I mean, it's such a casual kind of atmosphere. And I don't see enough black people here; I want to see more black faces around me.

Several black jazz musicians have come over here to live, in Copenhagen, in Paris, or elsewhere in Europe.

I wouldn't like that. I would like to come over and play and stay for four weeks, but that's good enough for me. I wouldn't like to go to places like the West Indies, places where you go for vacations. I like to live in New York and I don't want to be too far from there. Eventually I may leave and maybe go to California. I like California.

What do you feel and what can you say about the political and cultural situation in the States right now?

What's happening right now . . . it's funny but not funny in the sense of the word "funny"—a sad kind of funny that scares me to a certain extent. The things the government and Nixon and the rest of them are trying to do, the control they have over letting you know what they want you to know. In the schools there's a lot of propaganda. Like I was telling somebody the other day, I remember reading in one of my history books that Lincoln was one of the first people to free the slaves. But then they were showing you on the same page a picture of Lincoln sitting in a chair with a black servant holding a tray with a cup of coffee or tea. Because of all the propaganda, when you get your test paper you say that Lincoln was the first one, like you say that George Washington is the father of our country and that Columbus discovered America, but of course you know that the American Indians were there when he came. Myself, I really believed that propaganda then, which is sad. And a lot of people don't even pay attention to it, a lot of parents are not aware of it so they can't even tell you what's right. When I think about that I start to wonder what's going to happen. Personally, I don't think we will be here much longer. If things keep happening the way they are, this planet is going to cancel itself.

Just talking about pollution, I think they say that breathing the air in New York in the daytime is like smoking a pack of cigarettes—plus you have people smoking cigarettes around you! The food is out, you know; I'm just learning about different foods and what's good to eat. What's eaten is a lot of white sugar and white bread, white rice. . . . And there's nothing in it, no kind of nutrition. My teacher's telling me that if you're drinking a lot of cola, then you should drink an equal amount of milk because the cola does something to your bones; it weakens your bones. And you don't check it out until you're thirty-five. A lot of things are happening and are just out, it seems like everything is going right out. African culture is music and art, which I should know more about but I haven't had the time to really read about it. It's things like that I wish I had learned about in school. The white kids in school would be learning about people they liked to learn about and didn't interest me. So it seems you have to do these things on your own.

Jazz is a funny-sounding name, and I don't like it because of how people use it. I don't like labels anyhow. How can you label what is jazz and who plays jazz and who doesn't? I was talking to Gary one time and he was telling me that he considered Al Hirt and Stan Getz and musicians like that jazz musicians. These people gave the name jazz to the music they played. Like Benny Goodman, that's what they play—jazz. Myself, I play African rhythmic black culture, that's what I feel I can hear. Because in the music there is a message, whatever that message is. I can't even label it and the only reason why I would label it is to try to explain it to you. So I wouldn't call it anything. And when you ask me what I want to do with my music, I'll have to say that I want to make it meaningful. Not just to play, but whenever I play to have some kind of meaning behind what I'm doing. And mainly for my satisfaction, as I'm not that interested in what people think of how I play. I'm interested to a certain degree, but if I like it I don't care if you like it or somebody else likes it. I'm kind of forced to take that opinion. In the music so many different things are being expressed, like how you feel. So when people say they don't like what I play, it doesn't really make any difference to me. If I like something I like it, and if I don't like something I don't like it.

· 8 ·

Red Rodney

Red Rodney (1927–1994) went on tour with a big band led by Jerry Wald when he was fifteen and played with several other big bands in the '40s. Originally inspired by Harry James, Rodney heard Dizzy Gillespie and Charlie Parker and developed one of the most personal trumpet voices of bebop. During the years 1949–'51 he was a member of Parker's quintet, but drugs interfered with his career and for the next two decades he played commercial music in Las Vegas. Back on track in 1972, he proved to have lost none of his vitality. After a couple of years in Europe, he almost seemed to reinvent himself as a "new bebopper," playing—with Ira Sullivan, Dick Oatts, and Chris Potter, among others—a music that had its roots but also looked ahead.

Red Rodney, recently you did a concert here in Europe called The Musical Life of Charlie Parker. What do you think of this way of reviving Charlie Parker's music?

It's always a good idea, I think, especially for promoters, to capitalize on Charlie Parker's name. Unfortunately they weren't able to do that more when he was alive. I thought George Wein had a good idea, but I think there was not put enough into it. Maybe it was rushed, I don't know. The planning wasn't so good and a lot of things were left out. I don't think it was a good concert at all and it got progressively worse each time we did it. There was no continuity to it. . . . The good things were Jay McShann and the early music of Charlie Parker. I like McShann very much and I think we all liked playing the big band music. And then there was Dizzy Gillespie, always very good, always entertaining, always par excellence. But the rest of it wasn't too good, and none of us got much of a chance to play. I only played one small blues chorus and I played first trumpet in the big band. I don't know why they brought me over just to do that. The whole thing was a piece of commercialism; they tried to make some money and I hope they succeeded.

Previously published in *Coda*, February 1976

Talking about Charlie Parker's music, how do you value the things he did with strings at the end of his career?

Well, they were very nice but he felt very restricted with them. It was commercial and I guess they sold a lot of records—and that was good for him. But he didn't like it and after a while it drove him crazy.

Do you think that all the possibilities of bop have been exploited?

A lot of people say that but I don't know if I agree. Of course, there's always room for those of us who play that way to continue and to improve. I don't think that anyone has matched the greatness of Charlie Parker to this day. There have been different things coming out of his influence, John Coltrane for one, but it's my opinion that no one has matched him. I feel I can still play bop and be fresh and innovative. Coltrane came out of that idiom and he went on and developed a different way of playing. I liked many of the things he did, but at first I didn't quite understand. I had been out of jazz and away from it, and when I was confronted with that music it was new and strange and it sounded very harsh and unbeautiful to me. But after I listened a while I began to understand it better—and frankly I didn't care too much for it. I liked John himself but his disciples and those who joined in on what they called the free school. . . . I think there were a lot of hangers-on who were waiting for the ride and made a little money playing bullshit. I like anything if the guy knows what he's doing, if he knows the chords and knows his instrument and plays good music. It doesn't have to be bop, but when I hear somebody say, "Well, we don't play changes; we just play what we feel," and I see he doesn't know the changes and he doesn't know his instrument—then I know he's just joining for the ride and I don't like that. I think you have to know the rules before you break them.

In a Danish newspaper I read some comments you made on Ross Russell's book on Charlie Parker. How do you estimate the book on the whole?

I think it's great. Ross really researched his subject and today it's the best biography of any jazz personality and one of the best books on jazz. There are mistakes in the book, but they are honest mistakes. In the main it's an excellent book.

From reading the book one might get the impression that Parker was an unpleasant, even malicious person.

I didn't get that impression but, you see, Ross and Charlie Parker were not friends. However, Charlie Parker was not an unpleasant person at all; he was a very beautiful, pleasant, modest, and humble man who could laugh at himself and did many times, and he was very kind to all people. He had his moments, like anybody else, but he was a genius and also a very hedonistic person. He lived so wild and so precarious, on the brink of disaster at all times. It was amazing how he could even do the things he did in such a short life. But throughout history, a genius like that doesn't seem to be able to make it socially and straighten out his affairs—and that seemed to be Charlie Parker's situation.

I think that what Russell wrote about Parker was basically correct. Of course, different people would get different opinions of the man's personality and character. I knew Charlie Parker. He was very difficult to deal with—he couldn't get his personal life together and that was a problem. But he was very friendly. He was a liker and liked people and things; he was not a hater. Ross Russell also interviewed me, and I think he treated me very nicely. You see, I didn't know Russell. I met him way back, but I didn't record for his Dial label. I was out there in California with the Gene Krupa orchestra at the same time Charlie Parker was there.

In the book there is a chapter, "A Queer Night in Brussels," in which a certain incident is described. I understand that it was a mistake.

It was a mistake. The scene was true, but the whole thing happened in America. And Norman Granz didn't put us on a plane and sent us to the States; we were already in the States. I don't remember if we were with Norman Granz at that time or not; we could have been.

What happened to jazz after Charlie Parker?

That's a big question for me because I left the jazz scene at that time, and immediately after I went into commercial music. I was in Philadelphia and worked a lot of society parties, weddings, social events, etc. I made an awful lot of money, but the music was so terrible that I finally just decided that I wanted to play a little again. I moved to San Francisco and found that there was nothing there. There was less jazz than in Philadelphia, but being there I tried to make the best out of it and I played commercial music. It was a bad period during which I worked day jobs for a while and was completely away from the jazz scene. When I did hear some jazz it was when the free school and the modal things started, and I didn't like it. I didn't spend enough time listening to it, but my first impression was that I didn't like it at all. And as I kept hearing that kind of playing I thought that, well, maybe jazz has passed me by and I'm getting old and this is the new . . .

But as I listened more and more I came to the conclusion that this is not what I consider jazz. To me jazz is happy music—I feel the music must have a good swinging beat all the time. And when someone is playing his solos, his choruses, I feel he should play them the way he feels about life. Naturally, we do that whether we ought to or not, but it got so . . . angry, so far from what I think is reality. It became racial and when it became racial it became very bigoted, reversed bigotry. Now it was the blacks against the whites. And I think that was a bad slap against the white jazz musicians who had been the only people in America who had genuinely and sincerely not been bigoted. I didn't like a lot of the so-called new jazz I was hearing. The attitude, the performance, the music, the whole thing. And I noticed that the audience didn't care for it too much; they were getting bored. Saxophone players would stand up and play fifty choruses, which didn't make any sense to me. I'll quote Charlie Parker, who to me is the greatest. He said, "If I can't say what I have to say in three or four choruses I'll never say it." I believe that is still true today. I hear players stand up and play twenty choruses and they are just repeating themselves, saying the same thing they said in the first two or three.

You said before that jazz should express the happiness of life . . .

And the sadness. The good and the bad things, because jazz is after all an expression of what's happening to you.

But maybe some of the free players feel that these times are bad and therefore they have to put a lot of hate and anger in their music.

That's what they say, that's exactly what they say. I just don't agree. You know, Charlie Parker had some awful problems but he expressed them with beauty. In his music you can hear anger, sorrow, and you can hear beauty and laughter. He even laughed at his own situation. Charlie Parker was confronted with more adversity and more straight-out bigotry than the new young people. I think things have really improved a great deal. But of course they don't see this—how could they? I understand, at least I think I understand how they feel and why they feel this way, and to a great degree I agree with them.

But isn't the new generation more politically involved than the generations of musicians before them?

Well, that goes for their own political thought. They have no room for anybody else's and that I cannot agree with. No one is all right. . . . You see, I happen to be quite political. I have always been political to the point where I read two or three editorials daily. There was a time when I could name you every senator in the United States Senate and their affiliation and a great deal of their voting record. I can still give you a pretty good discussion about it although I'm not as fluent as I was at one time. Politics has always interested me, but many of the young people, I don't think they really know politics. They are just emulating the black power struggles and everything is blackness, blackness, blackness. But everything is not black or white—there's gray, there's blue, there's yellow—and I think they're losing sight of that. Of course, the Nixon period was an awful period and I hate to be the one to say "I told you so." But I did; I predicted it. Long before he won the election I predicted that if he did win many of the things that happened would happen. I think the American people deserved what they got because they got complacent; they turned their backs on everything. They were satisfied because their stomachs were filled, they had two cars in their garage, and they came home every night and put on their color TV and watched the cowboys and detectives—and they were satisfied.

But now, oh now they're worried because things are not the same. They should have thought of what a great man like Hubert Humphrey stood for. I don't think anybody could have stopped that war. I hated the war, but I do feel that if the working people had voted the way they usually do Hubert Humphrey would have been president and the situation might have been different, it definitely would. Nixon. . . . His whole career is showing what kind of man he is, and I'm glad we finally found out. I was very proud of the American people for ousting him; it's something I didn't expect and happily it did occur.

Speaking of American politics. . . . It's so different over there from the way it is here in Europe, and it's understandable. We were so big, so powerful, we've been so wealthy and so many things . . . and we're spoiled. We live in luxury compared to the average European, and like a spoiled child we can't see some of the other side of the fence. However, I think we're heading toward a socialistic type of existence and it's inevitable, just like it appears to me that the Soviet Union is heading towards a capitalistic type of existence. They're going to the right and we're going to the left, and maybe that is good. My own opinion now at age fifty. . . . At age twenty-five I was very leftist, more left than socialists, and I was embracing communism. But now twenty-five years later I'm much more conservative. I still like to feel I'm liberal, but I agree with the capitalistic system. I like it. I feel it could be improved upon and I think it should be. I don't think we should have poor, very poor, and I don't think we should have mass unemployment, but I don't think we are all the same and I don't think we should all earn the same.

But doesn't the capitalistic system mean that these things—at intervals—will occur? I'm thinking of mass unemployment, poverty, etc.

So far it has, but I think America has done more to eliminate these conditions than any other Western capitalistic country. If we will be able to avoid these things happening I don't know. I'm not that fluent and knowledgeable, but who is?

Every system has its weak points?

Of course, but I've seen a little bit of the other system now, including some of the eastern European countries, and I'm very proud to be an American now. Now that I've seen Europe, I really am. All I did before was to criticize our policy, our government, our ways. Naturally, not having seen any other ways it was so easy to criticize ours, and of course we're always so free to do that. But now I've been in places where you cannot criticize the governments. The people in the Scandinavian countries, in Holland, and in England are relatively free and can say what they want, but I'll have to admit that once I've seen a little of the other countries I'm very glad that I'm an American. I consider myself lucky I was born there.

We were talking about the jazz scene after Charlie Parker . . .

Yes, yes. I wasn't too enthused about the jazz that came after Charlie Parker. I realize that new music has to come in but I wasn't particularly impressed by the music that came after Parker. I loved Miles Davis, I thought he was most beautiful and he changed the sound of the trumpet. He made it much more lyrical. He was a great, creative jazz artist. What he is doing today, I don't care for it. I don't know why he's doing it and it doesn't matter why—he must have a reason. I like him, I think he's beautiful, and as for what he's doing now only time will tell.

Are there any of the new players you particularly listen to?

Freddie Hubbard I would naturally listen to. I think he's a tremendous giant, but now he's going in a different direction. I don't know how to label what he is doing. It's different from the jazz I'm used to and the jazz I like and feel. But he's so great—I've never heard a trumpet player do the things he does and he does it with such relative ease. He's beautiful and I love the way he plays. However, I prefer Clifford Brown, I prefer Miles Davis—that type of playing. I used to like Donald Byrd very much and I understand he's very successful now playing rock and roll. I've heard some people criticize him and of course when somebody makes money they are always going to criticize. And there's a trumpet player I just recorded with, Sam Noto, who used to play first trumpet with Stan Kenton and with Woody Herman. We worked together in Las Vegas; he's a great trumpet player. So this last recording I made, we called it *Superbop*, there were two trumpet players on it, Sam Noto and myself. We took Clifford Brown's solo on "Daahoud"—like "Supersax" with Bird—we harmonized it and played it, but unlike "Supersax" we each play our own solos. That album has just come out on Muse. Another trumpet player I would like to mention is Jon Faddis, a wonderful young player, a Dizzy-influenced player.

Let's go back some years. You started with the big bands.

Oh yes, I was with Jerry Wald, Jimmy Dorsey, Gene Krupa, Woody Herman, Claude Thornhill . . . there were so many. In Thornhill's band were Gil Evans, Gerry Mulligan, Lee Konitz. . . . It was a real progressive band. Gene Krupa's band was excellent—and of course Woody Herman; I was in the Four Brothers band. When I started playing my playing was more like Harry James, but Dizzy Gillespie turned me on to jazz. I lived in Philadelphia then and Dizzy was living there, too. I listened to him, and when he took me to hear Charlie Parker I was thrilled and we were friendly right away. And playing with him you will play your best, you'll play better than you can—and I did. I learned a great deal from playing with him every night. It has to rub off, some of it.

In Russell's book it says about you, "a trumpeter who would fit, who could play, who could follow directions, and who thought Charlie Parker was God."

Well, he got a little carried away there. I knew he was not God.

What about your musical situation right now?

It seems that I've gotten back into the jazz situation, and when I go back to America I hope to stay in the jazz field. I've gotten a little bit of publicity, so I hope to reestablish myself in jazz so I don't have to go back and do Las Vegas showroom orchestras and studio work. Of course this is very lucrative, but I don't want to have to do that. I'd rather be able to do twenty-five weeks a year playing jazz. That's enough; that would give me a living, and I'm going to try. That would be in the States, but I plan to come over here from now on every year for a couple of months. I have made some nice connections here, Arvid Meyer can always book me a tour, and there's Huset in Copenhagen to work. I hope to stay in the jazz field—too late for me to change now. Fifty years old, I'm gonna be chasing the bebops from now on till I go.

I have two albums out now, and another one is coming out on Spotlite. The recent album I already told you about is *Superbop*, with Sam Noto, Ray Brown, Shelly Manne, and Dolo Coker. It's out on Muse; it's a good one and they tell me it's doing very well. The *Bird Lives* album, which has been out for a while, was the first one I made since I was back playing, and I wasn't ready. I don't think it's as good as it could have been. The one I made in London on Spotlite with the Bebop Preservation Society was a great one. I love it and it will be out shortly. When I go back I'll do another one for Muse. I'll be recording quite a bit, like two or three albums this year.

You have been in Denmark for some time now and played with several Danish jazz musicians . . .

I've played with quite a few of the Danish musicians. I think you have some excellent players here. Your bass players are great; for some reason Denmark puts out great bass players. The two tenor players I've played with here are Bent Jædig—I think he's wonderful—and Jesper Thilo, also a very good player. I have played with both of them more than anyone. I have played with the two drummers Bjarne Rostvold and Ove Rex and your bass player Hugo Rasmussen. I like them very much. Of the bands I have worked with, I like Nissen/Fjeldsted the best because they have a modern book.

A lot of American musicians have come to Europe to live here. Would you ever consider doing the same thing?

No, I don't think so. I like where I live; I like America. I didn't know that before. I often felt that maybe I would like to stay. I hadn't seen Europe before, but now that I have I'm very happy to be an American. Not that I don't like Europe; I like Europe very much. I like to come here, to spend time here, and even live here a while, but I never want to give up my roots, my own country. It's the same here, like Bent Jædig. He has been all over Europe and has lived in Germany for years, but he's a Dane and proud to be a Dane.

The jazz situation in America right now and in the future?

What I am sure of is that we already have a large group of fans and this continues to grow, which of course is very good. Many jazz players are teaching in our colleges and schools today, which has opened up an entirely new and unlimited avenue of employment for us, as well as bringing forth new talent and giving these talents the tools and techniques of jazz playing. This will be very helpful to the students, and therefore more and more good jazz players will continue coming in. On the whole, I believe America is getting much better in the attitudes and respect for jazz and jazz musicians. Also we are earning more money than ever before, and I feel this will continue unless a worldwide depression hits us.

As to the future of jazz, I think it has a very bright future although there will be some hard and bumpy knocks along the road. Jazz will always be with us and as always it will keep developing new styles and conceptions. As long as the music is played well, no matter what the particular style is played doesn't really matter. . . . Just play it well and it will last forever because it is such a great artistic endeavor.

· 9 ·

Marc Levin

Marc Levin (b. 1942) studied at Rutgers University and with trumpeter Bill Dixon, with whom he also recorded. Before he moved to Denmark in 1973, he was playing with free-jazz musicians in New York: Alan Silva, Perry Robinson, and Leroy Jenkins, to name just a few. In Denmark he settled in Copenhagen, where he worked as a psychologist and pursued his musical career, working with Gunter Hampel, Mal Waldron, and others, as well as local musicians. In 1980 he left Copenhagen and the jazz scene. Today, still in Denmark, he is concentrating on his work as a psychologist. Levin holds an M.A. in psychology, works with NLP and hypnotherapy, and is composing music for various therapeutic contexts.

In 1956 I had a black teacher for the first time in my life. His name is Melvin Thompson and he has become a legend among the black community. Since that time, I think he has moved to Detroit. He was a little man with very big hands and he stood on a box in front of the orchestra. I wouldn't say that he was that much of a personal inspiration, but I was impressed that he could play all instruments. That was my basic start, and after that I took lessons once a week in the back of a music store for two dollars an hour. Then I met Allan Jacobs, who is also a teacher, and at that time I felt that he was a lot more sophisticated because he was from from the Jewish middle-class milieu, like I was. Allan Jacobs went to New York University when he was about twenty-four, he had played with studio bands, and he knew a little about Charlie Parker. He became my private teacher from 1956 to '58. He played clarinet, and in 1958 he felt that I was advanced enough to go to William Vachiano. Miles Davis and everybody studied with Vachiano, and I heard at that time that Vachiano had a lot of trouble with Miles Davis. Actually, I never got to study with Vachiano but rather with his assistant, John Ware, and in a way it was even better. John was a much cosier guy, very warm. I graduated from high school in 1958 and my family wasn't too supportive of the fact that I wanted to go to a music school, but they did help me.

Previously published in *Coda*, March 1976

It was a new school just getting started, and at that time I was not a very good trumpet player by those technical standards. They said that I had to move my embouchure, which meant I had to relearn the instrument. I had a rich uncle who wanted me to give up the whole thing and take a place in his stock trading firm and learn to be a stockbroker. I almost did that, but then I was listening to one of Bach's *Brandenburg Concertos* and I heard that trumpet player. . . . I had a close friend who began to speak to me and ask me if I wanted to be a musician. I wanted to be a musician because I was told in school that I wasn't intelligent enough to be anything else. I was a melancholy kid; all I had were my instruments and my Miles Davis records. Look at this—this is my first record. . . . It's here, my father bought it for me for 57 cents. It's Charlie Shavers and I still have it; it's a beautiful record. Now, this friend told me that I was intelligent and I could read books. And as he wanted to be a doctor, he wanted me to be a doctor too. He never became a doctor; he became a psychologist and I became a psychologist. and I'm just now becoming a musician again.

Anyway, that summer I read some books he gave me and I went to Rutgers University. I majored in psychology because my mother was in a hospital and I wanted to help her. My father was so relieved, and he did something that I think was pretty nice. He said, "I know music is important to you, and as long as you're under my roof I'm supporting you." So I studied with John Martell, a fine teacher and studio musician who lived in Bayonne, New Jersey, and in my last year at the university, where I was from 1959 till '63, I studied with William Gustenburger. At that time I began to get involved with avant-garde jazz. There was a guy named Peter Plonsky; one day he put his guitar down and began to play, and another guy fixed a radio so it would just go ooo, eee. . . . An early synthesizer. Bob Schectman played trombone and we would play things where I didn't have to know the changes. I remember there was a big, fat guy who had a part-time job at Savoy Records, and I had my little phonograph trying to keep up my record collection. One day that guy said to me, "You give me $1.25 and I'll bring you a modern jazz record." And that was the Archie Shepp/Bill Dixon Quartet, and I have that record here also. My copy, in fact, was stolen by a junkie, but I got another one. I put the record on and said "Holy shit! How can they get away with this? But they are making records, so they must be good."

But that trumpet player. . . . Here was Bill Dixon, who seemed to me to be playing the instrument the way it should be played. So I got Bill Dixon's number and I put it away, and then I came to New York one year later. One of my reasons for going to New York was to find Bill Dixon. I had finished the university in 1963, and for a few months I stayed in New Jersey because my mother had committed suicide earlier that year and my Jewish family told

Dexter Gordon, photo by Jan Persson

Marie-Ange Martin, photo by Martial Peres

Stanley Clarke, photo by Jan Persson

Duke Jordan, photo by Jørgen Bo

Benny Waters, photo by Jan Persson

Jackie McLean, photo by Jørgen Bo

Mary Lou Williams, photo by Jan Persson

Howard King, photo by Jørgen Bo

Red Rodney, photo by Jørgen Bo

Marc Levin, photo by Jørgen Bo

Warne Marsh, photo by Jørgen Bo

Mal Waldron, photo by Jørgen Bo

Ernie Wilkins, photo by Jan Persson

Sahib Shihab, photo by Jan Persson

Lee Konitz, photo by Jan Persson

Pierre Dørge, photo by Jørgen Bo

John Tchicai, photo by Jan Persson

me I had to stay with my father. But when my father after some time began to live a social life of his own, I was alone. I said to my sister that I never saw my father anymore and that he was always out. And my sister said that at least he would see me in bed when he came home. The ironic solidarity of the Jewish family structure.

After some searching I contacted Bill Dixon, but we didn't get together until March 1965. When I first lived in the East Village, it was a literary scene. Allen Ginsberg, Gregory Corso—they all lived there. Then around 1965 the painters came and in 1967 the jazz musicians began. I don't like to say it, but around that time also a lot of violence, the drugs, and other problems originated. My own use and abuse of drugs began in 1964 and ended in 1969, when I helped start the drug treatment program, Horizon House, in New York. I stopped using medium-hard drugs—cocaine, pills, etc.—in 1968, one year before.

What was happening musically when you came to New York?

You must remember all the time that this trumpet business was a very peculiar thing. I was discouraged from pursuing it as a career and I was told it was impossible for me. Also, I had no exposure yet to black people, really. I just met them on the street, but they were really kept away from me. And the white players said that I wasn't technically good enough. So I arrived as a young intellectual without being conscious of the fact that Archie Shepp, Bill Dixon, Cecil Taylor, Eric Dolphy, Freddie Redd . . . everyone was within one mile from where I was living. Now and then there was a little music going on I knew of, but I avoided going to the clubs because I didn't want to be disturbed. When I finally came to Dixon in '65 . . . now that I know him I don't know why he didn't throw me out of the house . . . but I came in not knowing that two years before he had said that he would never do another thing for a living except music, even if he should starve. I walked into his apartment and I said—"I'm coming to see you because I want to speak the language of jazz." He looked at me and said that he would take $4 per lesson. Also he told me to come back with some tapes of what I had been doing. So I got an old tape recorder and I made a solo tape. The first thing that struck me with Dixon was when the music was swinging, he wouldn't tap his foot and he wouldn't move his head; he would just sit and listen.

When I came back with my tape, he listened and listened and then he said, "When you're playing you're tonguing a lot . . . te-te-te-, and you don't speak like that all the time." And we began to talk about basic things of life. Dixon was a very fine painter; it was as a painter he began to get out of the ghetto. He won an art scholarship in the '40s, but he was drafted into the black army and he never finished it. But he made some paintings, beautiful paintings.

Now he gave me some strange exercises, and he would say to me, "Play that figure," and I would play it. And next he would have me to play the scale it came from. He would also have us play the same note and listen to each other. I came in to him one night and I just saw Dixon's back, and he was playing all over that instrument, up the high register, down the low, just whisper. There are a lot of trumpet players who can't do that, but Dixon had complete command of the instrument.

On my second lesson with Dixon, I had to bring another tape in and I got very high because I was scared. I found another musician, Max, and we began saying silly things and we played; he played clarinet, and I brought that tape in. When Dixon heard the tape, he listened, and I told him the whole story about my plans of being a psychologist. He said to me, "When you first came to me I thought I could make a competent trumpet player out of you. Now I think you're going to be a creative trumpet player and not a motherfucking psychologist or social worker or whatever you say you want to be." Dixon is very gruff, especially when he says tender things. Then he began to invite me to the Jazz Composers Guild to watch. At that time John Tchicai was living in America. Well, I met Steve Tintweiss, the bass player, and then after a few weeks I met Alan Silva, but I was very shy to go on the scene. Dixon was doing duos a lot with Alan Silva and I remember that Alan at that time didn't even read—he was a very intuitive bass player. And Dixon said to Silva—and he did it to me years later when I was pulling a band together for a record—he said, "Don't bother with stars if they give you trouble. Better take somebody who wants to learn and work with them." And he told me that Alan was forming a band and that he might be interested. So I went down and I came in, and in that band was the clarinetist Perry Robinson, who has become a great influence on me. Also there was Frank Clayton, who was my drummer for years, Ed Curran, who I made a record with, George . . . somebody who moved to California and the only one I didn't keep in contact with. I also met John Tchicai, but I didn't know him too well. We did remember each other, though, and I spoke with him when I was here in 1971.

Tell about the albums you made before *Songs, Dances and Prayers*.

They were all made within a few weeks. I think the first one was *Intents and Purposes* with Bill Dixon. I studied with Dixon for a year and then I played with him for a year. . . . Dixon had a pattern that I think is conscious to him because he did it with others. He taught them for a year, he had them work with him for a year—and then he didn't talk to them for a year. After that he accepted everyone as a peer. Dixon and I had done a lot of work with Judy Dunn, the dancer, and Dixon had worked at Newport that summer with Ken McIntyre and Bob Cunningham. When he was going to record his album I was hoping he would ask me to be on it, and it ended up that I was going to play percussion on his record date. Bob Pozar, the drummer on that record, is very technical; he taught me mallet technique and we built a whole percussion outfit. Part of it we called the midwestern white American tone block. I had a lot of tricks, where I had mallets in my teeth and so on. It was a very corny version of an African tone block. It was a beautiful record, done in October 1966, and the next one I was on was the record made by the Ed Curran Quartet a few weeks later. That group was seven or eight months old when the record was made, and to my feeling the quartet had been a little more cohesive in the beginning. By the time we recorded we were a little tired, disappointed, and uninspired in relation to earlier, although I think it's a nice record. Doing that record also reinforced my connection with Tiyoshi Tokunaga, the bass player, and I asked him to be on my *Dragon Suite* album. I liked the way he played, and it would have been a nice ethnic balance, and I thought very much in terms of ethnic balance at that time. Tokunaga was Japanese and he had a different opinion—he wanted to play with Bill Evans. After we made the record, we heard that Ed Curran went to a monastery and nobody's heard from him since. And then the next record was my album *The Dragon Suite*. That record and *Songs, Dances and Prayers* have many things in common. The idea was to show many different types of music. The first record is much less commercial than the next one. When I made *The Dragon Suite*, I had no sympathy for the jazz audience or anybody. I was angry; I was dirty and fucked-up.

What happened between the two albums?

Well, I had gotten a lot more satisfied, and it had a lot to do with my personal life. I stopped using drugs and began to find my place as a guest in the black culture. Over those years I began to understand a little more. I got hurt a lot of times, but not as many times as other white players because Dixon really prepared me to show respect all the time but still keep my dignity. So I was lucky working with some very fine musicians and have some good friendships. There were Leroy Jenkins, Muhammad Ali, and others. I learned much about black music and black culture because they were open enough to let me in. I was very close with Muhammad Ali, Rashied Ali's brother; he was really beautiful to me.

Songs, Dances and Prayers was released on your own label.

I told you that Dixon predicted certain trends . . . about Slugs, about a certain kind of change within the jazz scene. Dixon said in 1966 that musician ownership was the only alternative and that one day it would happen. He was talking about record companies, etc. Dixon also said, in 1965, that there would be—in some stadium somewhere—cheap jazz concerts available to a great number of people and probably sponsored by a beer company. He could see certain things. On my record he is credited on the back, and I feel he was pleased with it.

Why did you leave America?

It was a combination of different things. I didn't get much support from America as far as culture was concerned, and there were a lot of things wrong with the racial situation. Then I met a Danish doctor by the name of Jens Mathiassen. He wanted me to come to Denmark and work with the drug treatment system in Copenhagen. That was around June 1971, and we talked about me coming in September the same year, but that wasn't possible because they wanted someone who spoke Danish. But I came in the summer of 1972 and in the summer of 1973, and during that time we negotiated. Then I went back to New York and closed up my business and came back to Denmark.

Did you know Albert Ayler?

I knew Albert, but I was a little closer, I talked more with his brother, Don. The first time I saw Albert I didn't speak to him. He was with Henry Grimes and Sunny Murray, Charles Tyler, and Don. At the time it seemed very flipped and crazy, but I didn't say that to too many people. I was part and wanted to be associated with his music. But now as I look back, I realize it wasn't that crazy. I knew bop was not for me but I didn't know if I was ready for the other kind of music. The last time I saw Albert was a few weeks before they found his body in the East River. He was walking in the street and I picked him up in my little red Volvo. I gave him a copy of *The Dragon Suite*, and we talked about his brother and his family, the music scene, Bernard Stollman, and the ESP records. I didn't know Albert awfully well but I'm sure he wasn't the happiest guy in the world. However, he never struck me as being awfully melancholy or psychotic or manic-depressive (and I'm a psychologist, you must remember). I don't think he committed suicide. I think it could have been some kind of terrorism or something underworld-related or police-related. It may have been a racial incident that happened while Albert was taking a walk. I don't believe Albert was addicted to any drugs or was involved with anything consciously shady. I think he was killed—and I *know* he was killed in terms of the system. Another thing—there wasn't any police investigation of any significance as far as I know.

Which may indicate that the police . . .

Possibly, or else it's "just another nigger in the river." We must never forget this schizophrenic life going on. Charlie Parker is a genius to some and a nigger to others; that's how it is. Everyone thinks Leonard Bernstein is OK—except maybe the black people. But then there are more white people in the world than black people.

Do you agree that the type of music we could call free jazz has its limitations?

I don't believe we will ever be able to fly to the moon without a rocketship. Yes, we do have our limitations. In 1965 we had a poetry and music festival given by a poet who served cheese and sardines and wine on a pier. Frank Smith was playing with a drummer whose name I can't remember. The Electronic Duo they called it, but they had no electronic instruments. Frank was jumping up and down, honking and hollering, honk, honk, honk . . . and the drummer. . . . To me it was all the same. I'm not making a critical judgment, I want to avoid that, but really it was just one level of energy.

And while they were playing, honk, honk, honk . . . a little black Ford came down the pier. Very quietly the doors opened, and out stepped Ronnie Boykins and John Gilmore and Clifford Jarvis. Usually a Ford holds five or six, but there must have been around eight men coming out, and finally came Sun Ra. And then out of this little Ford came a set of drums and horns, and they opened the trunk and out came a celeste, and at the same time it sounded honk, honk, honk. . . . And these so-called savage niggers very calmly put down the celeste and put a beautiful piece of cloth on it. . . . Honk, honk, honk behind them. The black drummer, it was Clifford Jarvis, had a set of white drums and they all sat down behind their instruments. And when finally Frank Smith ran out of energy, Sun Ra touched the celeste very softly and began to play, and Pat Patrick and John Gilmore and all the men began to play so beautifully. What is structure? The Sun Ra band is a good example of a group that is so-called avant-garde, but it's very consistent and disciplined. And how often have we seen bop sessions where everyone's so fucked-up on dope and shows no responsibility at all. I personally have found limitations in bop. Frankly, I don't do it well myself. I don't think I'll ever play like Sonny Stitt, but now I have contacted Horace Parlan and hope I can study with him. I refuse to be made guilty that I have no right to make records, like a famous piano player once told me. He said I had no right to make my first record because I couldn't play *How High the Moon* in all different keys . . . that's just dumb. He was white, incidentally. I've never, ever been discouraged by a black player. When I've been discouraged, it's been by white techno-maniacs, not that all white players are discouraging.

If you ask me if there's anything I miss working with Danish musicians. . . . The attitude of the Danish musicians is very positive, and because they are not so suppressed, compared with the Americans, they don't have so many hysterical needs that have to be met, basically in terms of survival. They work hard, they usually have good instruments, and people like Erik Moseholm are helping very much by forming Nordic groups, etc., but I can still listen to certain Danish players and I can name the records from my collection . . .

I don't imply a weakness; I think it's built into this culture. Many Danes are into the business of self-effacement. Instead of drawing on their own culture, you get a bunch of halfhearted Zoot Simses and halfhearted Ben Websters. Therefore I think that a musician like Christian Kyhl is so important. He's considered crazy, but he is a true creator. He could go to New York and be respected. His music isn't that much based on American music—you can hear the Danish irony, the coziness, and everything. His music is beautiful. The Danish musicians have been very positive to me but I would like to see them trust themselves more. Then you would really hear something.

· 10 ·

Benny Waters

$\mathcal{B}$enny Waters (1902–1998) was a student at the New England Conservatory and became a teacher, one of his students being Harry Carney. He played and recorded with King Oliver and Clarence Williams around 1930, and during the '30s and '40s he did sideman duties with a number of big bands, among them Fletcher Henderson's, Claude Hopkins', and Jimmie Lunceford's. In 1949 he visited Paris with Jimmy Archey, staying there for almost twenty years and playing at La Cigale at Montmartre, occasionally touring around Europe. By the '80s he visited the U.S. regularly, and his vital, robust, full-blooded, Johnny Hodges– and Coleman Hawkins–flavored saxophone playing and entertaining vocals—almost forgotten in his native country—were greatly appreciated. Although he was blind by 1990, he continued touring and recording until a few months before his death.

My musical career started when I was six years old. I started on piano and went from there to other instruments. My brother, Clarence, was kind of a virtuoso. He played trumpet, clarinet, violin, saxophone, and other instruments, and he gave me a trumpet to play. I stuck with that for about two years but couldn't do much with it. Instead I went to the E-flat clarinet, and later I borrowed my brother's alto saxophone. He read music and he had a beautiful sound. . . . All my brothers could play something.

At that time I was playing mostly concerts at the private houses of rich people, just for music and dancing. I didn't hear any jazz until I joined a group in Philadelphia, where I worked with a jazz band led by Charlie Miller. We had an excellent trumpeter, we had a good drummer, and we had a girl pianist whose name I remember, Ruth Mossy, who was also excellent. This group worked together for about two or three years, and when I left I went to Boston to study music. I didn't study music until I was about 18 years old, and I had been playing a long time before that. I didn't study saxophone or clarinet; I studied just music, harmony, theory . . . the roots.

In Boston I worked with many of the great groups. Many of them may not be known so well, but one great pianist was Skinny Johnson and another

Previously published in *Coda*, October 1976

one was Walter Johnson. Then we had a conservatory graduate on piano by the name of Joe Steele, who may be the most learned, the most studied of all the pianists there, but I always gave Skinny Johnson the credit of being the greatest pianist of the era. I worked with another pianist, Tom Whaley, and we did concerts in the afternoons at hotels, and at night we played for dancing. It wasn't too much jazz; it was commercial deals. Also I worked many times with Johnny Hodges, who was born in Boston. I did some radio work for the Howard Clothing Company, a very big chain company that is still there. But, again, we didn't play jazz at all. We did classical solos—for instance, I played a number called "Saxofobia" written by a virtuoso, and the trumpet player did classical trumpet solos, etc.

That's where I got all my students, like Harry Carney. You see, people had not heard any Negroes play that type of music on the radio before, these technical things. Things like that were rare, and to play that kind of stuff you had to read music. And people listened and said—"That's the teacher for me." I had about sixty-five students in Boston, but I only remember one name, Harry Carney. Johnny Hodges didn't have to learn anything but to read music. He was playing more jazz than anybody else then. The first big band I worked with was Charlie Johnson's band, an organized big band. We had quite a good group—we had arrangements from everybody—and we had four arrangers in the band. I arranged and Benny Carter did; he was in the band also. We had the great trombone player Jimmy Harrison, and we had Dickie Wells with us sometimes. We had this little kid we brought from Philadelphia, Jabbo Smith, a fine player who was quite a success. With Johnson's big band, we started in Atlantic City, and from there we worked for a long time in New York, at Small's Paradise.

You recorded with King Oliver in the '20s . . .

Yeah, to be exact I did six sessions with Joe King Oliver and Clarence Williams. Williams had a publishing company, and they recorded all the songs they could possibly get together before the company was sold. Some of the recordings I made, I heard six months later. Others I have never heard, but you see I was working with Charlie Johnson's band, and recording with Oliver was just a matter of making some extra money. I guess you know that Joe Oliver's band broke up in New York. . . . Luis Russell later took charge of the band. He took the nucleus of that band and they had some great men there, but the band was nothing because they didn't have any arrangements. Everything was head arrangements, you know, and that's where I come in, about the idea of how necessary it is for a person to read music. They had some of the greatest soloists in the world in that band, but they sounded bad because they weren't reading. The musicianship wasn't there, but as for soloists they had them—Barney Bigard, Red Allen, J. C. Higginbotham—and they all went their own ways when the band broke up.

Head arrangements is a concept we also know from the Count Basie band at that time.

Yeah, that was practically the same thing—but that band didn't break up! Here's what happened to the band: Basie came to New York with some of the greatest soloists—Lester Young, Herschel Evans, Buck Clayton, Jo Jones—and the band was playing head arrangements. Head arrangements are always the same—there's nothing musical about them—but they swing. So the band couldn't compete at the Roseland Ballroom, where they were playing with bands like our band, Fletcher Henderson's band, and many white bands that played such music. There's a big difference there, so that's where John Hammond came in. If I'm not mistaken, the godfather of the Basie band is John Hammond, who paid for arrangements, etc., and everybody knows what happened. And John Hammond was the godfather of Benny Goodman, too. He also discovered many other guys, like Charlie Christian, and he suggested the Lionel Hampton/Benny Goodman/Teddy Wilson/Gene Krupa quartet.

But back to the Basie band. The band was always swinging, but you get tired of those head arrangements. So after John came, he lifted the band up. I heard Lester Young and Herschel Evans play "Moten Swing" or something like that for about an hour. . . . Of the two, I've always liked Herschel Evans's style better that Lester's. It was not that he played better, but Herschel played more soulful to me you see. I asked Jo Jones one day I met him, I think it was last year at the festival, and I asked him, "Actually, who was the best tenor saxophone player?" And I understood that Jo said Herschel Evans—and he should know. But you could not say that to those kids who listened to Count Basie's band. I'll give you an idea how popular Lester Young was. I was on the road with Charlie Johnson's band, and I went to a little joint where a whole gang of young kids played the jukebox. They played one of Count Basie's records and Herschel Evans was blowing, and all these young kids started, "Blow, Lester, blow, man. . . ." I told them that it wasn't Lester, it was Herschel. But they said, like, "No, man, it's Lester, don't tell me. . . ." And they were full of marijuana and they wouldn't pay attention to me. That's how popular Lester was. It was Herschel playing and he sounded good—so to them it had to be Lester.

You were not influenced by Lester Young yourself?

No, I was influenced by Coleman Hawkins. On alto I was influenced by Benny Carter, Johnny Hodges, and Earl Bostic. I played classical clarinet and didn't follow anybody much on that. I admired many, but . . .

After you left Charlie Johnson's band, you were freelancing in New York and also played for dancing . . .

Yes, that was during the Depression. It was a bad period for musicians and I was lucky I was working. I was playing for dancing and that was another type of stuff. I could read and we had music for every song we played. A lot of musicians who could play much jazz were out of a job because they couldn't read. This school where I was working was a high-class school. I'll give you an idea of how high-class it was. Do you remember that movie actress Barbara Stanwyck? That's where she came from, and the first movie she made was called *Ten Cents a Dance.* That's from that school. She was discovered there, as well as another girl. . . . I forgot her name. So it was real high-class; everybody was in tuxedos and evening dresses, and only white people attended the school. After Small's Paradise closed, I came to Fletcher Henderson's band. I actually worked with a lot of big bands, like Claude Hopkins. I rejoined Charlie Johnson and worked with Hot Lips Page and a Cuban band. After these bands, I joined Jimmie Lunceford; in fact, I was recommended by Claude Hopkins. When I formed my own group, we worked at the Red Mill in New York. I had a great little band there, very musical. I had a guy on guitar, Eddie Gibbs, who was one of the greatest unknown guitarists in New York. He had an electric harp and guitar, and this electric harp gave like a Hawaiian effect. We only had five pieces, but we sounded like eight because of this electric thing, which made it compact. I can remember my wife, Lorraine, on piano; the trumpet player was Herman Autrey, who used to work with Fats Waller; the drummer was Kaiser Marshall; and that's all. We played anything there—we were swinging with all kinds of stuff.

That was the beginning of the '40s, before I went to California. At that time the new jazz was coming up, Dizzy Gillespie and Thelonious Monk and those cats. I lived near Minton's and I had to go by there to go home, so I heard all the sounds. It was a harder style than the music I played and there was a little prejudice—even now there's a conflict about style. But I went there to listen, and Dizzy was terrific. I never heard Charlie Parker play there; Dizzy was playing that bebop music before Charlie came to New York. When Charlie came in, he was an asset to Dizzy because he was in the same vein. That's why they made those great records like *Hot House* and all that. I liked the music; I found it was great. Coleman Hawkins was playing progressive stuff then; he changed his style a little. Or let me tell you how I see it. Coleman didn't change his style; he was just playing bebop songs with a bebop flavor, but when he took his solos he played like he always did. Dizzy had a different style, different from all other trumpet players. Later on, of course, many people followed him, and Miles Davis came up and many others. But to me Dizzy was the most sensational—he had control and he still has . . .

I went to California in the late '40s. I went there to join my wife, who was working with me again, and I had charge of the band when that saxophone player, who was a Mexican, had to go to the army. That band I had was an entertaining band, the only band I ever had that was doing all the things the way I feel. We had everything going on—we even had big cowboy hats—we played mambos, we played tangos, rumbas. We had to do a certain amount of that stuff because we were near the Mexican border. On Saturday nights the place would be half full of Mexicans. Actually, Dizzy came to work on the West Coast but had no success. He flopped. Not because of him, but because of the rhythm. The young boys now are playing things that Dizzy has given up, things he used to do. I was at the Salle Pleyel in Paris and Dizzy was playing there. He had this great drummer playing with him . . . what's his name . . . Art Blakey. Art was playing so loud and Dizzy had to cool him down because you couldn't hear anything but cymbals all over the place. Well, of the bands I played with, from all standpoints, I liked Jimmie Lunceford's the best. Not particularly because of the music, but I like entertaining—as you've noticed. I do a lot of entertaining myself, and I like to work with a group where I can entertain. Jimmie's band had group singing, it had a quartet, a trio, and it had singing individually—and Ellington and Basie had nothing of that. So to me Jimmie's band was a better band, but not musically. I feel entertaining is important. Fletcher Henderson had a great band musically, but there wasn't any entertaining at all. With Jimmie we changed uniforms two or three times a night. I had fifteen uniforms, and things like that were important. We were in Kansas City and people on the corner were not talking about the music—they were talking about the uniforms. What I have said about the Jimmie Lunceford band can be proven if you listen to some of the records he made, like *Ain't She Sweet*, things like that.

In the beginning of the '50s I went to Europe with a Dixieland band exclusively to work for a month. But I stayed over here and the others went back. It was Jimmy Archey's band. I played clarinet and a little soprano, and Jimmy was the leader and the trombone player—the greatest trombone player maybe at that time playing Dixieland jazz. Henry Goodwin was the trumpeter, Tommy Benford was the drummer, Dick Wellstood was the young white piano player, and the bass player was Pops Foster. We did some tours in Germany and Switzerland, and I stayed and joined Bill Coleman. Why did I stay? Well, I guess just for adventure. I could have gone home to work in the States, but this was my first trip and I just wanted to se Europe. Like a little baby . . . for adventure. I had this job with Bill Coleman, and worked with him until I went to this little joint La Cigale in Paris. With Bill I played soprano and clarinet, and finally I bought an alto and we had Guy Lafitte playing tenor. When I left the band I went to this little place in Paris playing alto also. When the tenor saxophonist once went to Nice on vacation and didn't come back, the man asked me could I play tenor. I said I had no tenor but I had a friend bring over my tenor from New York. And I stayed on tenor. That's why I have all these instruments; that's how it happened. I came here with clarinet and soprano, joined Bill Coleman's band on alto, and changed to tenor at La Cigale. And I just kept all the four horns and use them as an attraction.

So I haven't been to the States for more than twenty years. The reason is that something is always coming up. I'm always working . . .

· 11 ·

Warne Marsh

Warne Marsh (1927–1987) started playing saxophone with the Hollywood Can-
teen Kids when he was thirteen, and Ben Webster and Tex Beneke were among his
first idols. His studying and performing with Lennie Tristano from 1946 through '52
and later reunions in the '50s and '60s shaped his musical thinking, to which he was
remarkably true throughout his life. Often, and unfairly so, accused of sacrificing the
music's emotional contents for intellectualism, he preferred working outside music to com-
promising, and consequently—aside from being a member of the five-saxophone group
Supersax in the mid-'70s—he mostly played and recorded on his own terms, except for
a few reunions with Tristano and Lee Konitz. Marsh was often labeled as the epitome of
cool jazz, but his playing contained a tightly executed cogency, rarely equaled in jazz.

As a child in Los Angeles, I played with kid bands. I started at about the age
of thirteen playing saxophone. We had a band called the Hollywood Canteen
Kids, and during World War II we played at the Hollywood Canteen—I suppose that was my introduction to jazz. I used to love Ben Webster and tried to
play like him. Those stock arrangements we played had chords, so that was my
introduction to what improvising is—when one is given a chord progression
to follow. But I can't say that really decided me to be a musician. What decided
me was . . . at 18 I was drafted into the army and posted right outside of New
York City. Charlie Parker was playing every night on 52nd Street. I had met
Lennie Tristano and started studying with him, and New York City was just
alive with music—a marvelous, stimulating place to be. The whole East Coast
of America was much more culture-conscious than the West Coast, much
more music-conscious, so it's fair to say that turned me on. Because that was
the time I decided once and for all that I was going to improvise music.

   In Los Angeles I heard Corky Corcoran, the tenor player, who also admired
Ben Webster a lot. I took a few lessons with Corky, but I only knew Ben from
his records with Duke Ellington at that time. We played a lot of Glenn Miller
arrangements, and I was listening to the original Glenn Miller records. The tenor

Previously published in *Coda*, December 1976

player and soloist on those records was Tex Beneke, and he impressed me and became an influence. I played the bass clarinet and clarinet, and I had previously studied piano, but I was a saxophone player from when I was fifteen, when I bought a tenor. Now I've learned flute and I play clarinet because I teach these instruments, but I consider them minor studies. Actually, any of the woodwinds is worth a lifetime career, and flute and clarinet are major instruments. I don't think you have time enough in your life to do all three of them well, so I play tenor and consider the other instruments as necessary evils.

Did you know Lennie Tristano before you came to New York, and how did you meet him?

I didn't know Lennie before I was sent to New York. I met him through a student of his, Don Ferrara, a trumpet player who was stationed at the same camp I was. My introduction to Lennie was through the correspondence he was having with Don, who was already studying with him. I was that impressed by how efficiently he made his points that I decided to go to him to study. The primary study is how to use one's ears, but that has of course been the truth in music since Bach's time. In Europe you call it solfeggio, and a good education starts with two years of solfeggio, which is all ear training. Before you're even allowed to touch an instrument, you must learn to think music, and basically I think that's Lennie's approach. A student is required to learn the rudiments of music in a manner that permits him to perform them without having to read music, you see, which an improviser needs. So there's no written music in Lennie's method. One must learn, for example, Charlie Parker's and Lester Young's solos by ear from the records and learn, first of all, to hear them in one's head—then learn to sing them, and finally learn to play them on one's own instrument. So it's . . . the major part of the study is to learn to think the language of music without having to read it. And then beyond that there are the meter studies, the rhythm studies, harmony studies, and complex harmony studies.

You also played with Tristano and Lee Konitz during that period.

Yeah, we had a band between 1949 and 1953, but during those years we were offered relatively little work, not really enough to keep a band together. Let's see . . . I think Billy Bauer was the first one to leave to keep working; he already had a family. Then Lee went with Stan Kenton in 1952, again because he simply had no choice. He had five children by that time, I think, and it was necessary to work. It wasn't until 1965 that we were offered enough work to keep the band busy, and we put the band back together then. We worked about nine months on the East Coast, but Lee felt that he wanted to be on his own, so we didn't stay together although there was enough work. I went back to L.A., where my people are. I had just been married myself and we moved back to L.A., and now here we are ten years after and things are coming together again.

Why do you think it was so difficult for the band to get enough work during your first period, around 1950?

Let me put it this way: bebop was in full swing and the main thrust of jazz was bebop. We were regarded as somewhat oblique, let me say—we were first of all considered being cool, even with the influence that we were intellectual musicians—which we really were. We were students of music; we were not interested in copying Charlie Parker and trying to play bebop. We were interested in being competent and well-trained musicians as a starting point, and then proceeding from there. That first band really was largely Lennie's work. The written material, the written part of it, was entirely done by Lennie. It was his band, it's fair to say.

Also, at that time there was a revived interest in some of the older forms of jazz . . .

Yes, but that remains current in America; it's always there I think. As a matter of fact, except for bebop I sincerely think that some of the best jazz is Dix-ieland. It's uncomplicated, honest, vigorous, stimulating music. And they play together—that's the big thing about it. There's not the kind of competition between the musicians you can hear in a lot of bebop and recently in all of the different styles of jazz that have emerged from bebop. Jazz, now . . . it seems that it has gone in twenty different directions since Charlie Parker's time. Jazz doesn't have just one meaning like it used to have. When I grew up it just had one meaning to me because Charlie Parker epitomized good jazz. Jazz was either bebop or it was traditional Dixieland, and that's all there was to it. You liked one or the other, you patronized one or the other, and now you have twenty different styles to choose from. And to my ears none of them are as substantial as either good bebop or good Dixieland—and of course the work Lennie did then. I think his music is as live today as it was then.

Around the time Parker was playing, you and Lennie Tristano worked together. Were the two schools of jazz very separate?

No, in reality there was a blend between the two. Parker recorded with Len-nie on a couple of occasions, and they liked and enjoyed each other. I myself worked with Charlie Parker. Lee worked with Miles Davis in that first nonet band—and very successfully. I love the way Lee played then. It was a period when everything was happening, and a thousand or so musicians in New York were really trying to do their best. It was simply a musical experience at that time—a growth in American music—and the emphasis was not being put on money and making success the way it is now.

You don't like the present situation?

I don't even think there is a situation. I don't think there is what you could call a musical community in America. In the '40s there was a community and in the '30s there was a community in Kansas City. Kansas City was a marvelous place for music, their clubs stayed open twenty-four hours a day, and Charlie Parker and Lester Young grew up there. In the '40s there was a center or a musical community in New York City, complete with an excellent audience. I think one of the best audiences in the world lived in New York. Now, that doesn't exist. There is no center. L.A. is just as active as New York is. I think there are more good performers and musicians in L.A. than in New York. What I'm saying is that L.A., which has never had a music of its own or produced major musicians or music, is now beginning to.

In the '50s there was a style or direction called West Coast jazz, played by people like Art Pepper, Bud Shank . . .

Art Pepper is an exception because he's a real musician. But I think what's called West Coast jazz usually impresses me as just a sort of watered down version of good New York jazz, a reflection of what was going on in New York. Certainly all of the musicians were congregating in New York during these years—it's just recently the trend is reversed and they are coming back to L.A.

About your own work now, you are playing with Supersax . . .

Well, Supersax . . . for about three years that's been keeping me pretty busy, and since it's an effort to re-create Charlie Parker's music, that means a great deal to me of course. That band will probably be active for another year or two, and is expected to come to Europe and go to back to Japan.

There's been quite a revolution in American music with the very young generation, which is tired of rock and roll. They find it is a poor medium for learning music—which it is—and Lennie and I, and I believe Lee too, are doing all the teaching we can handle. There's that much interest in finding out what really happened in the '40s. Good teachers in America are finding their hands full, and a good education is best available through private teachers. At colleges and schools there are courses for jazz, but it hasn't reached the level there that it can when it is taught privately—and this is jazz I'm talking about. Myself, I have as many students as I can handle right now—good students, good musicians. I teach them almost exactly what I was taught by Lennie. What you give a student really is an education that includes the disciplines of classical music. It's worthless to just give them ideas without giving them training. The student doesn't learn his music just because he's coming and taking his lesson. He learns his music because he practices the way classical musicians practice. The student teaches himself; that's the point, that the teacher is the guide.

So the classic studies in music—the rudiments of harmony, of meter, and of rhythm—can be taught pretty much as they are in classical music. Beyond that, when the student wants the contemporary knowledge of what's happening when you play jazz, which is to say what happens when four people get together and improvise. . . . You see, improvisation is not new to music. Improvisation was popular in Bach's time. Bach was a master improviser; Beethoven and Mozart were improvisers. A well-trained musician in baroque music was an improviser, but they did *not* establish a form of improvisation that had four musicians improvising together, which you could call ensemble improvisation.

It was the American Negro who did that, and the American Negro is entirely responsible for creating jazz. I give him full credit for bringing improvisation back to music. And I think it's the spontaneous playing of music that has revolutionized the world of music—it really has. The individual is once again given a voice in creating music. It's not all one composer and a whole symphony of musicians, with none of the musicians creating music but rather re-creating one man's thinking. Now we have again the situation where four men are thinking and hopefully playing valid music, improvising it together.

Speaking of improvisation, when you improvise on a tune do you play on the chord changes or do you have the melody in the back of your head?

Well, again, it's easy to draw a parallel with classical music. There's a form of classical music called thematic improvisation that exactly defines what we're doing in jazz. There's a theme and it is understood; it's the first chorus, and from there on that theme is improvised. There is a structure, in other words, as opposed to what is called free form nowadays, where the structure itself is supposed to be improvised. That's what's so hard about it—to be valid music there still must be structure. Without any structure it's random, and it simply doesn't qualify as valid music. Unless you like impressionism, which I don't. What's called free-form sounds accidental when it's good, but to me it sounds like a random attempt to play music. By accident you may hear good music, but I don't depend on that. . . . In the '40s Lennie, Lee, and I experimented with playing free music, and I think our first attempts were the most successful. In order to play that way, we felt that the musicianship had to be perfect and the results had to be valid music. But we stopped playing free music because the more we played the more difficult it seemed to be—and today we don't take chances like that when we play.

Do you agree with Lester Young's statement about the importance of knowing the lyrics to the tunes one plays?

Lester was an entirely lyrical person, and I know exactly what he meant. In fact, I think Sonny Rollins has made that same statement. Yes, I agree because that's part of what's being played. Improvisation is not music out of thin air. It's improvisation of a theme, and that theme . . . if it's *All the Things You Are*, it has lyrics to it. I think the improviser profits by being aware of the words as well as the melody. It's a minor point to me because words don't mean that much to me in music. I'm just an instrumentalist and I hear the melodies . . .

In your own improvisations and those of Lee Konitz, you have moved far away from the original theme . . .

We've extended it to a point where it may bear very little relation to the original. Nevertheless it's been logical stages. For example, Lennie's composition *Wow* is taken from a standard tune, *You Can Depend on Me*, I think. Charlie Parker wrote *Donna Lee*; that's taken from *Indiana*, so call it an improvisation of an improvisation. I haven't gotten to the point where I deny the theme—the theme is still there.

You mentioned the many directions of styles today. Which bands of today have moved you or impressed you?

In all honesty I have to say none. The good music played in the last 20 years has been by isolated individuals and not by groups. And naming some. . . . My most vivid recent musical experience is having heard and performed with Connie Crothers in concert in New York City last October. She is 34 and has studied with Lennie twelve years, and she is a fascinating musician. She is one of the three or four musicians I've played with who can evoke a better performance out of me than I could give were I playing alone. Niels-Henning Ørsted Pedersen is another one. Kenny Clarke had that effect on me, and I also have to mention Ronnie Ball and Sal Mosca. On the local scene in Los Angeles, I enjoy listening to Pete Christlieb, a marvelous tenor player whose father plays bassoon with the L.A. Philharmonic. There are some gifted piano players: Roger Kellaway, Mike Wofford, and Mike Lang.

Many of us feel that jazz is not valued as it should be in the States. Do you think jazz is so poorly estimated because it was created by the black American?

Yeah, oh yes. He's been regarded as a second-class citizen straight through. Charlie Parker was conscious of it, and he made a comment somewhere in one of the books . . . *Bird Lives*, I think. If Charlie Parker, Bud Powell, and Max Roach had been given full range to what they were doing, and if they had stayed together for five years, it would once and for all have established jazz as fine art. But it never achieved the stature of fine art in America. And yet it is. The saying went around when Bird died . . . well, Charlie Parker is dead now, and we'll get on doing our own little thing—and they forgot about him. Now there's a reemergence of interest in what was played in the '40s, an interest in what led up to bebop. And what led up to bebop was 50 or 60 years of honest music by the American black. His day is yet to come as a musician. The musicians in America know what's going on, but the people at large still regard jazz as folk music. That's a good way to put it—it's not art; it's folk music. That is what they think and it's stupid.

Unfortunately, I don't see the contemporary blacks in America doing much about it. There's certainly a lot of white musicians who have gotten the message and are taking their music just as seriously as Bird took his, and so we have a generation now of mixed white and black musicians doing a lot of different things, I have to say. The real achievement in American music is what led up to and included Charlie Parker, Bud Powell, Max Roach, Tommy Potter. . . . There are some other piano players, too, from that period: Kenny Drew and Duke Jordan. It's still the best music the country has produced, and it is still not given the understanding it merits. There are younger people now, though, who are beginning to study it and are taking their music seriously if they're not sidetracked by rock and roll, which is becoming passé. Young people don't want to hear about rock and roll; they want to find out what led up to it; they want to see through to the other side of it. They sense that rock and roll is relatively superficial music and it does not have the substance that bebop had.

By the time of bebop, the small group—the quartet, quintet, and sextet—had emerged as the forerunner of American jazz. That was the best context in which to improvise. The big band traditionally offered soloists like Lester Young and Roy Eldridge a chance to play sometimes, but the music wasn't really built around improvisation. It was still highly arranged, almost completely arranged with a few solos here and there. What emerged was the quartet. But Bird, Bud Powell, and Max Roach didn't work together long—they went out and got their own bands.

Big bands . . .

A big band today, to be a logical extension of good small group improvising, would have to build around the ideas of small group playing. In other words, the music would have to be very highly improvised. It sounds very difficult to put fifteen musicians together and get the same spontaneity you can get with four. It's a dream more than anything else; conceivably it can happen. . . . I think Woody Herman's big bands are the closest to being good jazz bands, and the early ones are the best ones. That's about as close I think a big band has to come to express the feeling that goes with small group improvising.

Woody Herman had some famous tenor players: Zoot Sims, Stan Getz, Al Cohn . . .

My buddies . . . well, they all played in one of the first bands, and it was an attempt to express the same feeling of a small unit. But Zoot and Stan and Al play small-group jazz now, and I do, and Lee does, so we're back to where we were twenty-five years ago really.

Duke Ellington's orchestra . . .

The Duke Ellington orchestra is a contemporary phenomenon. The band could only have happened in America during the '20s and '30s. When I was in my teens I loved the band, but just like all the big bands it ceased to have the importance to me that small groups do when I began to feel that I wanted to work in a small context. It offered more individual freedom.

During the '50s and '60s your public appearances were at times very few. Has that fact affected your playing?

No, not at all. I'll be a student of music my whole life. I miss performing, though; I think this is the most demanding form of art—not only to improvise, but to do it in front of a live audience. That's what jazz is all about: improvising. Let's put it this way—you're going to create the music, you're going to perform it, and you're going to do all that in front of an audience. That puts as much demand as I can think of on a musician; that's a challenge. Record dates I can live without. I did a studio recording recently, and it was not an acoustic recording; it was a mechanical recording. And when you divide musicians, when you place them 20 feet apart and try to record them through engineering, the musicians are not getting a blend in the first place. And there's no way in the world an engineer is going to fabricate good music from music that is not performed well. . . . And yet they seem to think they can do it. The whole philosophy is wrong; it's a product of our hi-fi psychology. They have sophisticated equipment; they have everything but good acoustics. But string quartets, for example, have not grouped in tight little circles for 300 years for no reason. They know what they're doing; they sit close together so that they can feel each other and they get the best out of themselves as a result.

Recorded jazz doesn't impress me at all, and the best performances are still going to be live performances when the band happens to be set up well and the club has some acoustics. No, it's a problem, and like all problems in music the only people who are going to solve them are the musicians themselves—by simply not allowing those kinds of recordings to be made when they are done track on track. It's manufactured music, not good musical performances. To my ears they're not; they don't move me. When we were recording in the '40s and the beginning of the '50s, it was a little more spontaneous. First of all, there was a three-minute time limit because we were working on 78s. Beyond that—we'll limit it to Capitol Records in New York—the recordings were done in a fairly decent studio; I don't even remember the mechanics. I don't remember if each musician had a microphone or if they recorded the room sound. They got a pretty good recording out of the music. However, records are always no more than second best; there's no way to get the complete impact of live music on records, hi-fi or not; it's just not there. So recording is incidental to me; it's a way of offering the music to a larger audience, but I never like to think of it as an end in itself. You notice that Lennie Tristano records very rarely. I do not listen to records very much at home. Occasionally I get out my Bartok and Bach, and that's really about it. Nowadays, that's what I'm listening to. I'm concerned with performing now, I want to get out to play in front of a live audience; that's what means something.

In Los Angeles there are two clubs where I do perform: Donte's and The Times. I work with my own quartet three or four days a month, and Supersax plays two or three weekends a month at Donte's. That's really as many personal appearances as any musician in L.A. is making. Los Angeles never did have enough of an audience to support live jazz—New York did. But jazz musicians do not make their livings in nightclubs any more. It's a period in jazz where everything is dormant, and I would even find it hard to say where it's going to reemerge. Right at the moment it seems to be more active in Japan and in Europe than it is in America.

Although you said you don't care for recorded jazz, can you name one or two records you feel will give a good example of your playing?

The recent Revelation record, which has my solos edited from an appearance at the Half Note in 1959. I think it's the best picture of my playing on record. And that's a live recording. That's the only record I can honestly say I think I've played my best on.

One tenor player we haven't talked about is John Coltrane. To many young musicians, he is as important as Charlie Parker is to others.

Your education would be complete if after you listened to John Coltrane you went back to Charlie Parker and really listened. Parker provided John with his start; just listen to John's earlier recordings. And let me say this for John: he not only loved Charlie Parker, but you can hear that he captured some of the willingness to improvise, to innovate. He really sounded like he was searching in his early career. He's a good, honest improviser. I enjoy him a little less than I do Charlie Parker. I feel John's best playing is his earlier playing, and I feel the same about Sonny Rollins. I enjoy John's ballads, the way he plays a ballad.

Coleman Hawkins . . .

Yes, I heard him after I heard Ben Webster, and I love him just as much. My own playing is quite different from both Ben and Coleman because when I heard Lester Young I said to myself, "That's it." Lester never wastes a motion; he's the most economical player I know—and that's art, that's artistic playing. Ben and Hawk are a little more emotional. The balance between emotion and substance is tipped toward emotion with both Ben and Hawk, but with Lester it's a perfect balance between emotion or feeling and the substance of his melodies—he simply never wastes a motion. We all know that his playing changed around 1945 in terms of efficiency or economy. He sounded healthy in the '30s and not the same later, and I can hear the same thing in Billie Holiday. They both performed perfectly for some years, and then something happened and their performances lacked the impact on me that the earlier ones did.

What does jazz means to you?

Well, it means improvisation. To me the best quality of our black music that we call jazz is its spontaneity, its willingness to improvise. As far as defining jazz in terms of style, I'm not particularly impressed by styles. Charlie Parker certainly had style, but that was a result of his abandoning himself to music—that's character. So if you take jazz as meaning American black music, then I don't care whether I'm regarded a jazz musician as such or not. But if you take it to mean improvised music . . . that's what important to me.

A final question. What do you devote your time to off the bandstand?

I have as many students as I can stand—thirty-two a week—and that's really a full load of teaching to me. And that's becoming a second career by now. I didn't take it seriously five years ago, but I do now. I feel that I've had one of the best educations available through Lennie, and essentially all I do is turn around and pass that on to my students. It's a fascinating career, really—teaching. To be given the responsibility for training the musician to express himself, not the old classical kind of teaching where you train a musician how to play Mozart . . . but to teach him how to express himself by teaching him to think the language of music . . .

· 12 ·

Mal Waldron

Mal Waldron (1925–2002) received piano lessons as a child and later graduated in classical composition, along with playing jazz on alto saxophone, an instrument he gave up after a few years. He played with Charles Mingus and Max Roach in the '50s and was Billie Holiday's accompanist the last two years of her life (1957–59). During the same time and into the early '60s, he was more or less the house pianist with Prestige Records and recorded with the legendary Eric Dolphy–Booker Little quintet, among others. He moved to Europe in 1965, living in Munich and later in Brussels, touring and recording extensively all over Europe and Japan. His angular and percussive playing sometimes sounds like a distant cousin of Thelonious Monk's, though rhythmically closer to free jazz than Monk ever was.

Mal, do you remember your first major jazz gig?

Well, it was about 1950 and I played with Kansas Fields and Ike Quebec. We played the Café Society, downtown New York City—that was my first professional gig. Before that I had been playing a lot of clubs, sitting in as an amateur musician. I had been sitting in at places like Minton's and at another place uptown in Harlem. You would meet people like Horace Silver, and many of the famous musicians would come up there, talk to them, and get to know them. And if they liked the way you played, they would offer you a job. I remember Dizzy Gillespie and Charlie Parker, Curley Russell, Allen Eager, Dodo Marmarosa, Ernie Henry, Cecil Payne, Fats Navarro . . . all the fellows. 52nd Street was a beautiful street because it had clubs right next to each other. So you would come out one door and go in the next one—you could hear Bird with Max Roach and go out and catch Bud Powell. All the cats were playing there.

I used to catch all the big bands when they came to the Apollo Theatre. They would come out to Jamaica and play theaters. I lived in Jamaica and heard bands like Jimmie Lunceford, Cab Calloway, Lucky Millinder, Count Basie, and Duke Ellington. Every week there was a new show and I would be right down in front of the line to buy my ticket.

Previously published in *Coda*, February 1977

I started playing classical piano when I was ten years old. I wasn't allowed to play jazz on the piano. My parents thought it was music of the devil. I got an alto saxophone when I was about fourteen, and I started playing it like a tenor. You see, I wanted a tenor but I couldn't afford it. I liked the sound of a tenor; the sound touched me humanly. I was listening to Coleman Hawkins, Don Byas, Lester Young, Dexter Gordon, Gene Ammons, and Chu Berry—all the tenor greats who were around at that time. All my heroes were tenor players. I started playing alto around 1941 and I gave it up around 1948, a little bit after I heard Charlie Parker. I couldn't keep up with him technically, so I stopped. I actually pawned my horn. I went back to the piano because I had much more technique on the piano to keep up with the new music. Bud Powell was my first influence, and after I heard him I heard Art Tatum. Duke Ellington was always a big influence as a piano player and as a composer. Then I heard Thelonious Monk and I liked the way he played—very sparse, very simple, very economical, and it appealed much more to me than Bud's playing. Bud was so flashy, those thousands of notes. . . . It overwhelmed me because my personality is not very flashy; my temperament is more introverted. So I went away from Bud and turned to Monk, and in between the two of them I found my own style around 1950.

In the beginning of the '50s you played with Charles Mingus . . .

Yes, I played with him from about 1954 until I left him in the beginning of 1957. It was beautiful to work with Mingus. We were like brothers; we were always like brothers—actually I saw him last week. There were tensions with some of the other fellows in the band, but I never had any tension with Charles. I have learned a lot about music from him. I learned how to play the piano from him because he corrected me and told me which things were not making it. He told the others also, but they didn't take it as I did. You know—their egos would get in the way and that's a very bad thing when ego gets in your way. You have to remember always to be humble, to try to learn something . . . and criticism, you must consider it and not just flatly put it down.

Later, in the beginning of the '60s, I played with Max Roach. In that band we had Booker Little, Walter Benton on tenor, Art Davis on bass, and sometimes Eric Dolphy was in the band, too, and also Clifford Jordan joined us. The band kept changing. No one musician just worked with one band at that time in New York; he had to work with several groups, and when he was not available they took someone else. The scene in New York around 1960 was busy, and I was working a lot. I lived in Jamaica and John Coltrane lived round the corner from me, and we were very friendly and visited each other and talked and discussed things. The music was very political around that time, but jazz was always political, always a protest against what was happening, against the status quo—but the freedom drive kind of put it more out in the open. And words were put to the music, words with protest.

I made four or five records with Booker Little and Eric Dolphy at the Five Spot; they were all made in one night. I knew Eric very well—he was a very warm and beautiful man; he always gave his all, and it was almost as if he knew he wasn't going to live very long because he worked so hard. He practiced all the time; he really worked hard to get a job done. I lost contact with him in 1963. At that time I was very sick; I left the scene completely and didn't see anybody except Max, who came out to the hospital to see me. But the others . . . I lost track of them all. I was away for about one year, suffering from a mental breakdown. And then in 1965 I went to Europe. I got the chance to write a motion-picture score for Marcel Carne, who came to New York to see me. He had heard the score I did for *The Cool World* and as he liked it he wanted me to write another score for *Three Bedrooms in Manhattan*. He asked me if I wanted to write the music in Paris or in New York, and I said Paris and stayed there. I went back to New York once to finish a score I had on order already, *The Sweet Love Bitter*, but as soon as I had finished that I went back to Paris. There was a lot of club work there; some of the clubs were Blue Note and Le Chat qui Peche. Buttercup Powell had a club, and I worked there. I played with Kenny Clarke, Ben Webster, and Jimmy Gourley.

Why I stayed in Europe? Well, it's a combination of things. Life over there, in America, is no life as far as I'm concerned. It's just an existence; most of the people just live to make money, just to have it, as an end in itself, and that's no life for me. And the artist is considered the lowest man on the totem pole—which puts me underneath the ground. As an artist you are appreciated much more in Europe. When I came here ten years ago, the music was a little weaker than it is now. It was good, though; it was shaping up. I stayed in Paris for about one year and went to Italy from there. I worked in Italy for one year, doing radio work in Rome also, and that was a beautiful job—making music all day. I traveled a bit and came to Germany and met a German musician, Christian Burchard, who plays vibes. He wanted to form a quartet, so I joined him. As he lived in Munich, I came there too, and as I liked being there I stayed.

Do you visit the States?

Yes, I go back every year for two weeks and it's as much as I can take. After two weeks I get on the plane—back to freedom. I went there last year to record and this year I may work. I don't feel too enthusiastic about working there because I know what it involves. It involves selling out to a certain extent, compromising yourself . . .

I have contact with Max and Mingus and with Don Pullen, Dannie Richmond, and Jackie McLean. I never seriously think about going back to the States, but I listen to the records coming from there. I like Miles Davis and

Herbie Hancock, and some Keith Jarrett and some Weather Report. I hear most of the records coming out.

Are you inspired by the young musicians?

I'm inspired by the young and the old musicians. I think the old ones have an edge on the young ones, though. The young musicians are more unschooled; they don't have the experience that the old ones have. The old musicians have much more influence on me, but I like to listen to the young because I may hear an idea that I want to keep to myself.

Has your music changed since you came to Europe?

Yes, it has changed because the situation has changed around me. The world has become more . . . seeking freedom. Everyone seems to be very much aware of freedom now, and that's what I try to express in my music. My music is much freer now, and I'm not tied down by chords and time and rhythm and form and harmony anymore. For instance, I don't play a tune with eight bars—eight bars—a bridge—and eight bars again. I don't play that as firmly as I used to do. I may stretch it out, it may go short, it may go long, there may not be any form at all. I like that way of playing, and when I go back to the other way I feel like I'm in prison.

Going back about twenty years, you worked with Billie Holiday . . .

Oh yeah, I worked with her from about April 1957 until she died in June 1959. It was beautiful and fantastic to play with her. She taught me the importance of knowing the words to a ballad before you play it. In her later years her voice was not as strong as it had been before, but it had a force that came through anyway, a very strong force. She was godmother of one of my kids. I read John Chilton's book about her and I feel it is a valid portrait that is very well documented.

You travel a lot.

Quite a lot, yes, always on the road as they say: Japan, all over Europe, Eastern countries too. I like to travel and I plan to continue doing it.

What are you being inspired by?

People around me, the scenery, and the atmosphere. Signs, different languages—all these things inspire me. And Japan, going there and playing there has been very inspiring, too. . . . Japan is really a jazzman's paradise. The jazz player is so well known that he's like a movie star in America. When they see him in the street, they crowd around him and want his autograph. He's like a king; it's a fantastic ego trip in Japan. They have many clubs in Tokyo filled with musicians and people every evening. I think there are about thirty clubs functioning with live music and there are other clubs called jazz coffeehouses, where you can hear your favorite jazz records while drinking a cup of coffee. When I go to Japan, I play concerts mostly but also clubs. I play solo, and I play with Japanese musicians as well. Let me name one: Kemiko Kasai, a girl singer over there who is very affected by Billie Holiday. She is only nineteen years old, but still she has so much to tell, so much experience—and when she sings it's like she's much older.

Your musical situation right now?

Well, I live in Germany and I work all over the world, traveling all the time. I am composing all the time, too. I compose at least one tune a day. More tunes actually come to me every day. I don't practice too much at the moment, because when you practice you have a tendency to play what you are practicing, which means you're going to be held in more, instead of being as free as you could be. That's what I'm striving for now—freedom. Recently I've been working with Marc Levin. We came together the first time I came to Copenhagen, and he helped me out, helped to find me some work. We got along beautifully, and it was a natural thing for us to start playing together. In the future I'll try to be as free as I can, more free than I am now. Also I would like to see more of the world. I know a lot about the music of Africa and would like to see Africa, and also visit Russia and South America.

What does jazz mean to you?

It means to me a modern expression—a way of speaking, communicating with people in terms of today. The vocabulary has to be from the moment, from what's happening now. I hope my music will change in the future. Jazz is very important to me, and I think it should be taught in schools. That would introduce the music to the young kids—many of them don't even know of jazz. They hear what's on the radio, which in mostly the other type of music, pop music. Jazz should be given a programmed education in schools. Also, if the music could be given some more time on radio and TV, it would give people a chance to hear jazz and they would like it, many of them.

Do you prefer working in clubs or do you like playing concerts more?

I enjoy both, but I prefer concerts because your music will reach more people. In clubs you usually play for two hundred people, but in a concert hall it may be thousands of people, so you will reach a larger audience. But the concerts have some drawbacks as people are sitting there facing one way, while in a club they move around and the atmosphere is different. A concert hall is very much like a studio except the people are there. But in a way you feel you're playing to a space as you don't see people out there in the dark.

You have made many records. Could you name one which is representative of your music?

In fact I can think of three: *Meditations* is an album of piano solos, *Mal Waldron with the Steve Lacy Quartet* is an album I did for America Records and Steve Potts is on it too, and finally a trio album, *Impressions*—an old one but still one of my favorites.

· 13 ·

Ernie Wilkins

Ernie Wilkins (1919–1999) learned piano and violin and studied music at Wilberforce University. In the '40s he worked with the Jeter-Pillars Orchestra and Earl Hines's last big band, and in 1951 he joined Count Basie's orchestra and put an unmistakable mark on Basie's sound from then on—more so as a composer/arranger than an instrumentalist. After leaving Basie in 1955, he still gave priority to composing and arranging in a style that contained elements of swing as well as bebop, knitted seamlessly together. His writing was very much in demand by Clark Terry, with whom he often played, Dizzy Gillespie, Sarah Vaughan, Dinah Washington, Harry James, and Basie, among others. Wilkins had a rare ability to write for vocalists in a way that seemed to almost enhance their qualities. He settled in Copenhagen in 1979 and formed his Almost Big Band, which lasted until he was incapacitated by a stroke in 1993.

Forming the Almost Big Band and writing for it as a composer and arranger is the best thing I've ever done in my life, in my entire career. It has made me happier than anything else I've ever done. I started the band in the early summer of 1980, and we got our start playing at Jazzhus Slukefter in Tivoli here in Copenhagen. Well, there's a whole lot more to it than that—actually my wife, Jenny, put the idea in my mind about forming a band of this size. I called it the Almost Big Band because it's a twelve-piece band, but actually it *is* a big band. I was trying to come up with a good name for the band rather than just Ernie Wilkins and His Big Band or something like that. So I came up with the Almost Big Band because the band is a little smaller than the conventional big bands, which can be from seventeen to twenty-two pieces. When I came here, I had brought a few arrangements with me from the States written for a twelve-piece band, and after getting the idea from Jenny I started writing

Previously published in *Coda*, February 1984

a whole lot of new music because I didn't have nearly enough. I built up a repertoire by writing new music, which I'm still doing. When I thought I had enough music to perhaps form a band and start playing somewhere, I started getting the musicians for the band, with some help, of course. I got a lot of help from Richard Boone in finding the different guys for the band.

Since 1980, each year seems to be getting a little better for the band as far as work is concerned, especially during the summer. Everybody knows that it is very difficult to keep a big band working, even an Almost Big Band. It is a sign of the times also—the economy. The band has American musicians who made Denmark their home and Danish musicians, and it's working out fine. It's been great from the beginning. All the members of the band are top musicians and the musicianship is quite high, but it's not just the musicianship. It's the spirit, the dedication . . . we're serious about playing the music, but we also have a lot of fun, which is so important. There's a big difference between having a good professional band and having a great band. I think I have a great band with a high level of professionalism, along with the spirit and dedication and the good feeling. I consider myself very lucky to have all this going for me.

I must brag a little bit, too. I'm writing, composing, and arranging better since I've had this band than I ever did in my life. I like what I'm doing now and I think that I'm more creative and a little more adventurous in my writing. I take a few more chances harmonically, rhythmically, and melodically, and I think it's because of the inspiration from my band. When I write for the band, my approach is similar to that of Duke Ellington's. It certainly helps when you have constant personnel with musicians like Jesper Thilo, Bent Jædig, Sahib Shihab, Kenny Drew, Richard Boone, Jens Winther, Erling Kroner, etc., etc. When I know those guys will be there, I certainly consider their particular gifts when I sit down to write. Before I formed the band, of course, I was trying to do my best when I was writing, but now it's for me. Every time I sit down to write, I think about the members and who should I feature on this particular one, etc. It's a challenge and it's fun at the same time. I even sit there and try to hear in my mind, like Bent Jædig playing a solo on this tune, or it might be a tenor battle between Bent and Jesper Thilo, or maybe I might feel that Per Goldschmidt should play a baritone solo—or maybe I should play something myself. From one arrangement to the other, it's altogether a different approach and it's really unplanned. I think of these different things as I go along.

We have two albums out. The first one was for Storyville, and our latest one is for Matrix Records, which is co-owned by Kenny Drew and Sahib Shihab, who are both in my band. The band is much better all around on the second album than it was on the first. The band was still very new when we recorded the first album in a studio. I really think the difference between the two albums is remarkable. Also, recording live in front of a very enthusiastic audience sure helps. And to be honest, I think this is one of the best live recordings I've ever heard, especially by a big band.

From the present, let's go to the past.

My mother tried to get me to study piano when I was a kid, but I wasn't too interested. Finally she bought me a violin for a Christmas gift, and I liked the violin and was taking lessons. However, by the time I got to high school, my friends—one was a saxophone player and one was a trumpet player—were into jazz, and as I wanted to play jazz I didn't want to play the violin anymore. And, Roland, I'm sorry that I stopped playing violin. I should have kept playing violin till today because I think I would have been a great jazz violinist, but that's one of my few regrets as far as music is concerned.

I was in the navy for three years during the war. Fortunately I was a musician and could play saxophone in the navy band, and although we had to play marches and the concert band stuff, we still had our jazz going. After the war I was discharged in Chicago, and for a little while I stayed around Chicago, which was really jumping at that time. It was a fast city and everything was happening there. Eventually I went back to St. Louis, my hometown, because one of the local bands wanted me to join them. But at that time Earl Hines was trying to keep his band together—this was 1947 and big bands were almost dead as I guess you know—and Earl had me come from St. Louis to Chicago to write for this band, and eventually I played with the band, too. It only lasted a few months before he had to break up the band, and that's when he went with the Louis Armstrong All Stars. After that I went back to St. Louis again and played with local bands. One band was led by a guy named George Hudson—Clark Terry was an alumnus of that band, which was very good. In fact, I think it was too good so we never did do much. Finally, after fooling around St. Louis, gigging around, waiting tables sometimes to help have some money in my pocket. . . . In fact, I was waiting tables during the week for my father, who was a headwaiter at a private club, and gigging on weekends. I wasn't too happy and wanted to get out of St. Louis and kept thinking about New York City, that magnet. Then in 1951 Count Basie decided to reform his big band and he asked Clark Terry to help find some fresh faces, some younger musicians, and Clark told Basie about me.

So my brother—Jimmy Wilkins, who is a trombonist—and I went to New York and joined Basie's band in May 1951. I only stayed with the band for four years, and I say only four years because when you think about Freddie Green and some of those other guys, four years is nothing. Things were pretty bad those days, even for Basie, and when we went out on the road there were a lot of places where there were more of us on the bandstand than there were people in the audience. It was kind of rough going through 1951 and '52, but somehow Basie kept us working. The salaries weren't very high, but then we started recording for Norman Granz and gradually things started picking up. We played at the Savoy Ballroom before it was torn down, and then we found a home—Birdland—and that was the beginning of a success story, Basie's come-back. Especially after Joe Williams joined the band and we had a hit record, *Every Day I Have the Blues*—which was my arrangement, by the way. Several people were writing for the band, Neal Hefti was writing some great things, and we got Frank Foster and Frank Wess, who were writing too. Thad Jones came into the band and Thad's music was very modern, very . . . oh, it was Thad and how can I put it? The things he wrote for Count Basie were so good and so modern that Basie wouldn't play them. What I'm trying to say is that what Thad was doing in Basie's band was a sign of things to come. And you know the story of Thad's and Mel Lewis's band.

As for myself, I think I was writing too much when I was with Basie; I was really spreading myself too thin back in those days. Frankly speaking, ninety percent of the things I wrote then, not only for Basie but for whoever else, I really don't want to hear any more. Only a very few things I did in the past I can sit still and listen to. Right now I just want to hear what I am doing now—that's all that interests me, and I've been waiting to say this for a long time. After I left Basie, I did a lot of writing for different bands, and one was Harry James's band. Harry wanted his band to sound like Basie's band, and of course they couldn't. I did manage to write a few things for the band that came off all right, but finally I remember writing Harry a letter. I told him that I would try to be myself and just write for him, and that he should stop trying to be like Count Basie. And sure enough, the later things I did for Harry were much better; there was much more creativity in them.

In 1956 I made a State Department tour with Dizzy Gillespie's band. Dizzy was forming a band to make a Middle East tour sponsored by the State Department, and Quincy Jones was helping to form the band because Dizzy was out of town. I was busy freelancing around New York and very tired, and Quincy knew it. So he called me and asked me did I want to go on tour with Dizzy's band. He said, "Why don't you come with us; you need a break any-way," and that's how it happened. I wrote two or three arrangements for the band—Quincy did, too—and we also had a trombonist and composer, Melba Liston, who was writing for the band. Not only did we play the Middle East; we also played Greece and Yugoslavia, and it was one of the most interesting tours I've ever made. One of the reasons why the tour was so great was that wherever we went—whether it was Beirut, Damascus, or Karachi—we were able to be there for at least a week, so it gave us a chance not just to play every night and relax with the music, but to see the country and meet the people and get to know them. Those are the things that made the tour memorable to me. I shall never forget it. One little incident I vividly remember was after we finished a week or so in Pakistan. We were boarding the plane, and people were all around the fence that surrounded the airport and they were all crying—they hated to see us leave. You can't forget a thing like that. There was one little guy who was playing a homemade violin and who had played for us all the time we were there.

And playing with Dizzy, of course . . . I can't describe it. All I can say is that he is the most electrifying bandleader I have ever worked with. When he gets up on the stage in front of a band, there's electricity and you want to play like crazy—because of him. Dizzy is incredible and he was in top form on that tour, reaching heights that you didn't even think that he could reach. So when you're sitting there, you have to be very careful that you don't forget to come in when you have to play some background or ensembles—and sometimes you get so mesmerized that you forget to come in. I've done a lot of big band things with Diz since then, and through the '70s it seemed like at least once a year he would form a big band just for a special concert, and most of the time I was called to play with the band. And each time it was the same kind of experience. I really hope one day we can do an album together—Ernie Wilkins's Almost Big Band, featuring Dizzy Gillespie! I can dream, can't I?

And let's not leave out Clark Terry, because that was an experience, too. Clark is another one of those musicians you can listen to and forget about everything else. He is also the kind of bandleader who can light the fire. I started playing with Clark's band around New York in the latter part of 1968 and played on and off with the band until 1979, when I moved over here. Only a few times he was able to keep the band together for several weeks or a month, but when I first joined the band we were playing every Monday night at a place called Club Baron in Harlem. We were there for about a year every Monday, and that was rather consistent for those days. The band also played for a long time—again on Monday nights—at the old Half Note, and we made a European tour in 1973. That tour included Copenhagen, and that's when I met my wife, Jenny, who had booked the tour. Can you believe it's ten years ago already? Ten years ago.

During the '70s I was also doing a lot of college and high-school clinics and jazz workshops. I was also appearing as a guest soloist at different universities, colleges, and high schools, and that's where I made most of the money. At the same time I was still writing for an occasional recording session, doing occasional commercials for the radio, and teaching, too. I also played jazz clubs with my own group and was working with Clark Terry's quintet besides his big band. A variety of things kept me busy before I came over here. When I moved to Denmark in '79, I had planned to have my home here, but I had also planned to commute back and forth to New York—but it so happened that I've only been back to New York twice since I've been here. It turned out that way although I had definitely planned to spend at least as much time in New York as I would spend here. The reason it turned out this way is mainly because of the Almost Big Band, but of course I have to make a living and the band just doesn't work often enough . . . unfortunately. I would like to be able to make a living just working with my band.

I can tell you about a lot of things I've been doing since I've been here. I've done writing for radio bands all over Europe. I've worked with the Danish Radio Big Band and Etta Cameron, and with the radio band in Rome in 1979. And then, in the last couple of years, a lot of my work has been with amateur bands here in Europe. I had some music that I brought with me, and I have written a lot of music that I can use with these amateur bands because they can't quite come up to play pieces that are too difficult.

When it comes to other arrangers and composers, I think Gil Evans is great. I've known Gil Evans and his music ever since the late '40s, and all I can say is, well, seeing all these polls in *Down Beat* and other magazines, they have two categories, one for arrangers and one for composers. And they always seem to stick Gil Evans in just the arrangers column, and I resent that because he is not just a mere arranger because you can call a guy who writes for circus acts an arranger. Gil Evans is not just an arranger, and I'm not either, and neither are Thad Jones and Toshiko Akiyoshi and Slide Hampton or any of us. We are composers, too, and I wish to emphasize that. I resent those two categories. I have to name some other composers and arrangers who I like very much. Of course Duke Ellington and Billy Strayhorn were a category by themselves, but now they're gone, so let's speak about those of us who are still here. I mentioned Gil Evans, Slide Hampton, and Toshiko already. Others I like are Frank Foster, this guy in Canada, Rob McConnell, Bob Brookmeyer, and one who has been very much neglected, Gerald Wilson, but let me end this by saying there's nobody greater than Thad Jones. He's an incredible writer.

Well, I want to put some shit in the game now. I love all those beautiful people I've mentioned, but now—since I formed the band—finally I'm my own favorite arranger and composer. But only since the last three years, and the way I'm writing today, after forty years in the business, I'm almost pleased, *almost.*

The future for the band and myself? Well, to be realistic we can only work fairly consistently during the summer with the festivals, etc. We just can't do much during the rest of the year, that's the way it is . . . so I plan to spend more time in the States. I intend to go over this fall, and I'm in the process now of setting up things and have written so many letters that I've got writer's cramp. I must spend more time in the States because there's not enough happening here. Things are bad over there, too, but I think I can do okay for like three months and work consistently and make some good money. The reality is that I must go over there. This will still be home and I will still have my Almost Big Band. It's awfully difficult to make a living over here unless you're working for TV or the radio as director or whatever. . . . A lot of the bands I've worked with in Sweden, for instance, they have had to cut back on their budgets considerably and they are not getting the same amount of money they used to for hiring people like Thad Jones and myself. The whole world is suffering from the recession. I don't know exactly when I'll be ready to go to the States; I think it will probably be after September when things start in the schools. I recently heard from my good friend Clark Terry, and he's got some things for me to do. If I get out to Detroit, where my brother Jimmy lives, he's got some things lined up for me to do there. Jimmy has his own band and has had it for over twenty years. But, as I told you, Denmark is going to be my home from now on. Even if I go back to the States for a period of time, this will still be home. Only if I was very young I might consider to go back to live. But now I can't pull up my roots anymore.

And finally let me say this. The Almost Big Band is the only band that I'll be writing for from now on; I won't be writing for any other bands. I would like, though, to do special projects such as the arrangements I did for Kenny Drew recently, using strings, woodwinds, and brass. I would also like to do some movie scoring. I did one film score back in 1962 and I didn't know what I was doing, and the film wasn't good and neither was my music. I've learned a lot since then, but even if I got an assignment to score for a film I would still study with somebody who's totally experienced in film scoring. I wouldn't let happen to me what happened in the past. It just didn't come off good at all. The title of the film was *Stand Up and Be Counted*, and they never showed it in the major theaters, only in the drive-in theaters and on late-night television at four o'clock in the morning! So no more writing for dance bands. I'm writing for myself. I'm my own writer and it's lasting. I'm doing it for me, not for anybody else. All my life I have helped others become great, but that's in the past—it's all over with. This is a new era, thank God, and it's time for me to help myself become great . . .

· 14 ·

Sahib Shihab

After playing alto saxophone with Fletcher Henderson and Roy Eldridge, Sahib Shihab (1925–1989) became friendly with some of the beboppers and played and recorded with Thelonious Monk, Art Blakey, Tadd Dameron, and Dizzy Gillespie. He did a lot of session work during the '50s and came to Europe in '59 with Quincy Jones' Big Band in Harold Arlen's show Free and Easy. He stayed in Europe, most of the time in Copenhagen, and worked with the Clarke-Boland Big Band, the Danish Radio Jazz Group, Thad Jones' Eclipse, and Ernie Wilkins' Almost Big Band, recording with all of them. In 1965 he composed the score for a jazz ballet based on the folktale "The Red Shoes" by Hans Christian Andersen. In 1986 he returned to the U.S.

I always liked music and wanted to play an instrument. In the beginning I was very lazy and wanted to find an instrument I could play lying down. My mother bought me a saxophone but you couldn't play that lying down, so that was the end of that dream. I had a teacher, Elmer Snowden, who used to play guitar with Duke Ellington but who also played the saxophone. I had him as my tutor for about three years. I was still in school in upstate New York when I had to go south to bury my mother, who died around that time. I stayed for about one year in Savannah, Georgia, working with Larry Noble and his band. When I came back to finish school I was around sixteen or seventeen years old, and I joined Buddy Johnson's big band. Buddy had a singer who made a tune that became quite popular. I think it was called "Baby, Don't You Cry." This was during the war and the singer got drafted, and as I was the only one who could imitate his sound I got up there and sang.

From Buddy Johnson, I went to Fletcher Henderson. I think I joined him in Chicago. That was my first experience playing lead alto and it scared the pants off me because it was the first time I ever saw so many sharps . . . all those sharps! But I made it and wound up making advances very quickly. At that time there were so many places in Chicago to play, like Club DeLisa and

Previously published in *Coda*, October 1985

the Rhumboogie Club. Chicago was also where I began getting some experience conducting a band. Roy Eldridge was working in a place called El Grotto, and as he was going back to New York I joined his band because I wanted to get back to New York. At the Apollo Theater in New York, I played with a lot of bands. You know Art Blakey—before the small bands he had the original Jazz Messengers, which was seventeen pieces and a heck of a band. But it was hard to keep a band of that size together because of the economic situation, and the guys began to leave because there wasn't enough work. Tadd Dameron had a band at the Royal Roost in New York with Shadow Wilson on drums, Curley Russell on bass, Tadd of course on piano, John Collins on guitar, Miles Davis on trumpet, J. J. Johnson on trombone, Cecil Payne on baritone, myself on alto, and a tenor player from Brooklyn, Ray Abrams. When I worked with Tadd, I met Harry Belafonte for the first time. He was singing that type of balladeer thing and we never thought he would make it because he sounded too quiet, and people like to hear something boisterous or something manly, like Billy Eckstine.

During that time, the late '40s, people began to recognize artists like Thelonious Monk. When I first played with Monk, he fascinated me. Something about his music was hypnotic, and he created an atmosphere of his own where he would go. He was so advanced mentally that a lot of times he would get in trouble with the police because he would say things that were so completely out, according to their way of thinking, that they couldn't understand him and would say he was crazy. Monk's music was complex. It was out of the norm and everything out of the norm is always complex when you first see or hear it, but you have to give it a chance—and once you sit down and look at it, you find out it fits. I understood the man, and when we recorded I always considered him as just another cat. I mean, you play the music and if it isn't right you play it again to get it right. He was straight to the point and I enjoyed working with him. He was beautiful because he would also rely on the other person's intelligence. I also found his way of playing the piano very amusing; he was an act and kept me laughing all the time. Most of his dancing he did over here in Europe. A lot of musicians learned from Monk because he was so unconventional. As for myself, I learned a lot harmonically; he opened my mind up to experimentation, and I don't remember hearing him play the same thing twice. Monk was a genius. I think I was with him, on and off, for about a year. Idrees Sulieman was there too. Then it was Art Blakey and his small group and other groups. Living in New York I made a lot of recordings with different people. I was musical director for Dakota Staton for a couple of years, and I was with Illinois Jacquet, a strong cat who is still playing good, for another two years, I think. I traveled a lot with Illinois, and it was while I was with him that I came to Europe for the first time. Coleman Hawkins and Sarah Vaughan were also on that tour. I have really been in good company all my life.

Working with Dizzy Gillespie was another beautiful experience. I don't know how he got his name, but it fit him. He was beautiful, a heck of a showman, and he could play! Working with him you could be so fascinated by his playing that you would feel like a customer. And Dizzy had a sense of wit that carried him through, and he took care of business much better than a lot of people. I also worked with Charlie Parker on a few occasions, and he was the one who told me to go on and play my horn no matter what. I remember one time I was with Art Blakey. We had to make some extra money and we would give dances on Sunday afternoons up in the Bronx. We would select a star as an attraction, and this particular time Charlie Parker was supposed to play with us. Among the members of that band were Monk, Art Blakey, Ray Copeland, Cecil Payne or Leo Parker on baritone, and I played the alto. We were supposed to start at 3:00 and people were there waiting to hear Bird, who hadn't shown up. At 3:30 Bird still wasn't there. What happened to Bird? But we started playing, and fifteen minutes later we looked up and there was Bird coming in and getting up on the stage. "I'm not gonna read no music," he said, and I told him that I would read the music, and when it was time for him to solo I would give him a sign. Bird tore the house down, and naturally—New York being what it is—the audience wanted to hear an alto battle, and I didn't know what to play behind Bird. He looked at me and said, "Sahib, all you can play is what you know." And that's what I did and people accepted it, and Bird too.

The late '40s and the early '50s was a fantastic period. Birdland was there, Bop City, Basin Street . . . all those places. So much was happening in New York. A fantastic era . . . rich, rich, rich. Unfortunately so many musicians died as very young men. Somebody said that's the trouble with getting old—that all your friends die. If that's the case, then I think you have to make some new friends. John Coltrane is another giant I played with. I recorded just one date with Coltrane for Prestige, but every time I go back to the States I run across someone who remembers that recording. It was a certain passage I played on the baritone that stays with people. That same year, 1957, I also worked with Coltrane in Art Blakey's big band and could hear what kind of musician he was.

I met Quincy Jones before I worked with him. I came in contact with Quincy around 1959 through Jerome Richardson about the show *Free and Easy* that Quincy was putting together to take to Europe. Quincy was arranging Harold Arlen's music and it was kind of an experiment, incorporating musicians on stage with the actors. We were going to act, too; we had costumes and everything, and it was fantastically done. The music was great. We rehearsed in Brussels, and because we had to act also we had to memorize all the music—and it was a two-and-a-half-hour show. It took a lot of rehearsing, but we made it. I don't think I'll ever be able to anything like that again. The show had a Sportin' Life type of theme, and many of the scenes took place around racetracks and clubs, incorporating that 1920s milieu: callgirls, jockeys, playboys, pimps, and racketeers. We performed in Holland and France, and the last place we played was in Paris where the show folded—because of bad management, I think. We had a band meeting to find out what to do. We knew that if we went back to the States we would be out of work, so we might as well stay over here, which we did. In order to keep the band together, I think Quincy went $65,000 into debt. He was asked some years later if he was going to put a big band together again and he answered, "If I do, shoot me!" In general, the show was well received because it was a new thing, and if it had ever gotten to New York it would have played a long time there.

Another person I want to mention is Walter Gil Fuller. A fantastic man. I trusted him and he taught me a lot, not just about music. He was such a business-minded man and I started selling real estate with him—I got myself a real estate license because of him. I learned a lot from that guy, but now I can never find him. People used to put him down because he had so much upstairs, so much knowledge.

The first saxophone player I listened to was Willie Smith, who was with the Jimmie Lunceford band, a marvelous band. I liked Willie Smith's playing and the way he would lead a section. Benny Carter was another influence, but on baritone I had no influence because I started playing it by chance. Diz had this baritone player, Bill Graham, and he was going to leave. Diz told me to buy Bill's baritone, which I did and that's how I started on baritone. At that time of course Bird and Diz were my strongest influences musically, that style. Right now, today, I play more alto than anything else with Ernie Wilkins. I like to play alto in a section and I like to lead, but as far as solo work is concerned I like the baritone. It takes a certain type of mentality to play alto, to play it right, and I don't know if I have that. I like to play the baritone because I have been able to do with the baritone something I haven't heard anybody else do, even people like Harry Carney. I like to produce a sound that I can stand myself. When you listen to Duke's band, you can always tell if Harry Carney was there. He had a particular sound, a sound that to me wasn't soft enough. On the other hand, Gerry Mulligan's sound is too soft, too light. There was another baritone player, Leo Parker, who had a good sound. I like what he did and I like what Cecil Payne is doing. I think that a baritone shouldn't be harsh; it should be something you can hear without putting your fingers in your ears.

I'm beginning to go more and more to the States and I'm hoping to get a grant from the government, from the National Endowment for the Arts. If I get that I'll go over there and do whatever I have to do for the grant. Twenty years ago I wrote a ballet based on Hans Christian Andersen's *The Red Shoes*, a jazz ballet. I submitted excerpts of that toward getting this grant, and if it comes through I would like to reproduce that in the States, and would like to use Max Roach's daughter's group. Maxine belongs to a group called the Uptown String Quartet, and I would like to work with them and some of the other musicians over there. The ballet was performed here in Denmark.

I came to Europe for the first time in 1954, and it made such an impression on me that I wanted to go back and stay because it was hard for me to believe that people could be so nice. I thought that maybe they were just nice because they knew I was only here for a minute. . . . It was five years later I came back with Quincy, and after the show I told you about, Quincy got some work over here and we made a tour of Sweden, too. I was sitting with the others—and I'll never forget this; it was in Paris, in April—and the guys told me to get up and catch the plane, to get out to the airport . . . and I just said bye and decided I was going to stay right here. I stayed in Paris for a little while and then went to Sweden, and after two and a half years in Sweden I came down to Denmark and I've been here ever since, more that twenty years. When I came, working conditions were good, things were happening, and I was new—I hadn't become a local. I started writing here in Denmark, composing, which I hadn't done much in the States. When I first came I worked with the Radio Jazz Group and with some other groups. Oscar Pettiford was here, Niels-Henning Ørsted Pedersen was a teenager then but playing great, and I played a lot down there at the old Montmartre and at Vingaarden.

Around the time I came to Denmark I ran into Gigi Campi of Cologne, and he wanted a baritone player for the small group they had—called the Golden Eight or something like that—with Kenny Clarke, Francy Boland, and Benny Bailey. The band grew and became what was known as the Clarke-Boland Big Band. It was a fantastic band and I worked with it for about ten years, the longest I ever worked with a group of people. And Campi was the first impresario I met who treated musicians in the right way. I always stayed in contact with him, and actually I just finished doing a project called Music Unlimited. But in the meantime he was working on a project, I don't know how he came into it, with the Pope. As a young priest the Pope wrote poems, and now recently the Vatican gave him the rights to have music put to these poems. He took about ten of them and gave them to the Italian composer Tito Fontana, who does a lot of music for theaters and stuff like that in Milan. To put music to the Pope's poems was a very difficult job because the poetry is more like prose. But Fontana wrote the music, and he got Sarah Vaughan as one of the vocalists and a fellow named Bernard Ighner as another. Now, Bernard Ighner was the one who wrote "Everything Must Change"—I think it is his most popular song. Francy Boland orchestrated the music, which was written by Tito Fontana and Sante Palumbo. Gene Lees did the English adaptations of the poems, and Sarah and Bernard did the singing. Plus we had six voices from England, and the strings and woodwinds of the Rundfunk Symphony Orchestra conducted by Lalo Schifrin, *and* a big band consisting of 22 musicians. We recorded the work for TV in Düsseldorf, West Germany, a few weeks ago and I think it was a success. By the way, I did all the copy work, which was a lot of work because the music was orchestrated for 72 pieces. At this point the tape is being mixed, and the record should be out sometime this fall.

Now I'm more interested in writing than I am in playing. There's so much I would like to do, and I'm in contact with some boss composers like Quincy and Thad Jones and Ernie Wilkins. I can get the same satisfaction out of trying to put something on paper and imagine what it will sound like. It's a feeling that's difficult to explain. As for the future. . . . Well, the two projects I have told you about: the ballet music and the Pope project as I call it. We're supposed to go to Brazil and Argentina with a handful of the key men in the band and pick up symphony players wherever we go. And that has to be coordinated with Sarah and Lalo. I have an equal amount of interest in both projects because the Pope has a message. He is a good man, and part of his message is incorporated in his poems. Working with this project and being a part of it was a beautiful feeling and a lot of labor was going into it. The work is titled *One World, One Peace*, a commentary on the time we live in . . . like we're ready to blow up the whole thing. I think it has a good message, and I think it will help also because I saw the reaction of the people down in Düsseldorf.

I listen to the young musicians of today, but a lot of it isn't jazz. They're playing—I don't know what you want to call it—Johnny Griffin calls it march music. I listen to it and if it's good and it moves me, I don't care what label you put on it. I think a lot of folk tunes are beautiful, and there's only one type of music and that's good music—bad music, forget about it. I don't like to stay in just one vein. I've worked with so many different musicians and in so many musical contexts, and I can play all of that stuff, you know. Free jazz is the only thing I don't particularly care for. I feel that in order to be free you have to know what freedom is; otherwise you don't know what you're doing. When I first picked up the saxophone, I didn't know what I was doing—that was when it was free jazz! But after going to school and learning what it was all about. . . . I think those guys are just playing protest music, and to me it doesn't make much sense. I think Bird was so advanced that they haven't caught up to him yet, and after him came Coltrane. I think that music will outlast this century—if not more.

· 15 ·

Lee Konitz

In his late teens, Lee Konitz (b. 1927) met the pianist Lennie Tristano, whose teaching and thinking influenced him strongly. He recorded with Tristano and Warne Marsh in the late '40s and again at a few reunions in the '60s and '70s, played an important part in Miles Davis's Birth of the Cool band, and was with Stan Kenton from 1952 to '54, by which time he was recognized as the only entirely original counterpart to Charlie Parker. From the early '50s he regularly toured and recorded in Europe in a wide variety of settings, from solo to big bands, from straight-ahead to free jazz, and he has for many years been much sought after as a teacher. Over the years the emotional spectrum of his music and his tone have broadened, but his phrasing has retained it long, arabesque-like lines. He was awarded the Jazzpar Prize in Denmark in 2002.

Lee, what does jazz mean to you?

It means an opportunity to do what I do best, and that includes traveling around and creating music every night. It means creation at many various levels, from just the slightest bit of creation to big areas of creation. That's just what the meaning of life is to me, creation in some form or other. We all have some special way of creating a little space or a big space of our own if we want to. It means a very big responsibility, and I have spent my whole life trying to develop this ability that I have to create in this way, and I intend to spend the rest of my life doing that. Now I have been able to do it long enough so that I understand that this process of creating is available to anybody who is interested. Jazz traditionally has been talked about and realized as a creation of the black people, and white people are just kind of inheriting the music at best. I like the feeling that it's a much bigger process. It's for anybody to do, but I understand that black people have to emphasize sometimes the importance of their contribution because most of the time they don't get enough credit for what they have done. The music and the process, however, are much bigger

---

Previously published in *Coda*, October 1986

than all that, and I'm very happy that I have been able to continue to live my life this way. That's part of what jazz means to me.

Looking at the whole history of jazz, I see it as a very important and continuing valid music. The best part of that music will remain valid and real and part of the whole development of the improvising art. Earlier today I was speaking with the American pianist and composer-arranger Butch Lacy about the young people, and the responsibility that those of us have who are older and have experienced the process of this music. Butch was pointing out how some of the teachers and students here in Denmark are not fully ready to accept the tradition of the music, the American Negro tradition. I think at this point more people are getting away from that obligation in some way, trying to offer a more individual contribution to the music. I understand that, but it doesn't work that way. The students have to know what the tradition of the music is, in jazz or in classical music, in order to do their own thing eventually. The tradition of jazz is our Bach and our Beethoven.

Your first job playing jazz or jazz-influenced music was with the Claude Thornhill band . . .

It was my first real experience in that type of a situation, traveling around. I mean, I had been with so-called dance bands before, briefly, but this was the longest period of traveling. The band was a beautiful ballad band. The arrangers were literally teaching some of the older musicians how to phrase bop music. Being a member of the band was a special experience, the feeling of being in. I wish that I had been a little more able to play comfortably during that period, but I was still learning and still a little bit . . . the word is impetuous. I remember Danny Polo, the beautiful lead clarinet player in the band, who was an older man. He was able to see where I was at, and he knew how to kind of cool me out when I got a little bit too impetuous—he was really a very lovely man. As I said it was a beautiful, a thrilling ballad band just playing straight dance music, and we would be playing these magnificent Gil Evans arrangements with two French horns and a tuba. I don't know who originally suggested the idea of the unusual instrumentation, but I just read a piece someplace saying that the sound of that band was Claude Thornhill's and that he just tried to make it as interesting as possible. So that sounds like it was his idea, but somehow I have a feeling that it was Gil's idea.

Who were your own influences on alto?

The first people I listened to were Willie Smith and Benny Carter, but Johnny Hodges was probably the strongest influence. I think I've always had a very special feeling for a ballad, and Johnny was a very sweet ballad player as you know. But I liked very much Willie Smith and I was listening at those times to the Harry James band, which Willie was playing in then, and Benny Carter of course, especially on some of the records with Roy Eldridge and Coleman Hawkins. It was later that Charlie Parker came on the scene, and it took me a little bit to get to hear that music. It was a bit too much for me at that time. Lester Young came a little later, too. Around 1945 I was working with one of those dance bands led by Jerry Wald, and there was a beautiful Lester Young-type tenor player on the bandstand. Stan Kosow was his name, and I remember going to his room once to hear some Lester Young records and the music really made an impression on me. Those were basically the people who I was enjoying in jazz, and I also heard a lot of nice big bands that were being broadcast on the radio at that time. Then eventually I would meet Lennie Tristano . . .

You talked about your own playing in the Claude Thornhill band, and you said that you were still learning at that time. Listening to your solos on the recordings you did with Thornhill, it sounds like you already had your own personal style by then.

I was able to make a sound and have some understanding of the things I had been studying, but there were still some very essential things missing in my musical education. The actual delivery of the music was still not in the right place to me. There was an indication, which thank goodness was picked up by some people who encouraged me to go on and develop that. That's the way I've always looked at it, as an encouragement, and when I listened to my music I heard the imperfections in it—there was something I needed to develop. My first teacher was Lou Honig, and I didn't pick him out. He came with the clarinet lesson plan that I got, and he turned out to be a very nice man who helped me to learn how to blow the instrument for the first five years. I also studied with Eddie Harris when we were growing up in Chicago. Then I studied with another man named Santy Runyon, who was a very fine saxophone player, a very clever mouthpiece maker, and a very good teacher. And it's funny—over the years for some stupid reason whenever I would have an interview of some kind the attention was generally on Lennie Tristano. He was the man who was most influential in my music development so I never thought it that important to mention Lou Honig and Santy Runyon, and then I found out that they both were deeply resentful and hurt that I never mentioned them as my first teachers. So I'm taking this opportunity to mention them because they were both really very influential. They taught me the process and the principles of blowing a horn. And Santy actually got a little bit into some kinds of improvising materials, but it didn't seem that any of that really came to any serious point. I was just interested in playing; I didn't have any real goal as a soloist until I was encouraged by Lennie to do that.

There was also one situation in Chicago at a time I was playing with a band led by a man who made clothing for many of the jazz bands. They would come to Chicago and buy their uniforms from him. His name was Harold Fox, and he had a band that was made up of some of the good musicians in Chicago, black and white, and we used to play a lot of the black bar rooms in Chicago, like the Pershing Hotel. I even sang the blues and some ballads—like Al Hibbler—and I was just a little guy with funny glasses. I never mentioned Jimmy Dale, Harold Fox's artist name, in any interviews for some reason until a few years ago, and I got a very angry letter from him—he's now living in Florida—saying, "How come you never mention me? I gave you your first chance." And I thought to myself that I had been very selfish never to mention Jimmy Dale in connection with my development. I hardly ever sang again after that; it was my first time, and he encouraged me to sing. Then one year I played at Carnegie Hall at one of George Wein's Newport Festivals in a program devoted to Chicago jazz, and I told the rhythm section, at one point, to just play the blues behind me, as I wanted to pay tribute to someone in Chicago. Joe Williams was the M.C. that day, and before we went on I asked Joe what was the last line in "Around the Clock Blues" and he told me. So we played the concert thing with Ira Sullivan, and we played a couple of numbers that didn't make it very well. Then I started to make this speech to say that one of my early influences was Jimmy Dale, and that I would like to pay tribute to him. I finished the speech at the beginning of the blues and started to sing one chorus of "Around the Clock Blues," and my voice slipped up one octave. My wife was in the audience and she told me I sounded about fifteen years old. Joe Williams came out at the conclusion and asked me if that was what I wanted the lyrics for, and he said 1-2-3-4- and *he* sang and saved the show. Joe Segal, the man who has been responsible for a lot of Chicago jazz, was in the audience and he was going to Florida to visit Harold Fox. So the word got out, and I received a very nice letter and an apology from Harold. It took me about thirty years to get around to it, but I tell you I sometimes forget things.

In an interview some years ago, you talked about Lester Young and how his playing has changed many lives . . .

Yes, I certainly know that he did. I just love the space Lester Young created. I don't know how else to really say it, but it also included his sound, his rhythmic feeling, his melodies, his whole attitude about making music. It was just as free spiritually as it could be. The complete goal, I think, of this kind of creation is to get out of ourselves for a moment and into. . . . We each have our own universe that we function in, and then we try to relate to another universe, and then we have the total universe that we're all moving around in. The more of these universes that we can contact and kind of link up to the total universe, that's the goal in communicating we're trying to reach, I think. And Lester was no longer just a nice, dark-skinned man who was wearing a funny hat—he was like a spirit. I didn't know exactly how to look at it then, but I'm sure I felt similarly when I first heard him.

On this trip—this is my second month in Europe—I'm playing each night with different people, and fortunately in this music you can do that. The spiritual part makes up for the imperfections of not having played together before, and for a moment here and a moment there it can happen. And whoever can hear and experience that is in for a special experience. For a minute they can stop thinking of Gadhafi and about nuclear weapons and all that, and become involved in a spiritual thing. In a way I feel like some kind of traveling evangelist or something—the Billy Graham of the saxophone. I mean, I don't intend to do that. I just go out and play, but I'm certainly aware of the nature of the communication when it's working. With Charlie Parker it was the same spiritual force as with Lester Young, and even on a higher level in some ways—and then in some other ways I liked Lester even more sometimes. It was the same idea, the same area that they were able to occupy at their best. I didn't know Lester really but to say hello, and I spent a little time with Bird and had a little trouble just relaxing with him at the time. But Bird was very nice and gentle to me, and I remember one little incident, among others, when we were together on a Stan Kenton tour. Bird borrowed ten dollars from me, and after a week I asked for it. The band was just coming up on the bus one by one, and the first guy who came up, Bird said, "Hey, give me ten dollars." And when he got it, he slipped it to me. I seem to have a recollection of sitting in with Bird two times at a club. It was very strange, but I better not say anything about it because it was strange and I don't know if I can make the right picture now. All I can tell you is that I think Bird sincerely thought I was missing out on something by not listening to him like everybody else was. On the other hand, I think he had a very deep respect for Tristano, I think that's very well substantiated by now. He was trying to know Lennie and learn where he was coming from. And every time we met, he would continually say that he was glad that I was doing my own thing—and of course that was always an encouragement, too.

How did you actually meet Lennie Tristano?

By accident. I was working with one of the dance bands in Chicago. I think I was fifteen or sixteen, and I went across the street where a friend of mine was playing. Lennie was in the other band, which was like a kind of rumba band. We got into communication immediately, and I knew that this was my opportunity to seriously learn something about the music. I think Lennie was always very concerned that he'd give me or whoever was studying with him the right point of view so we could develop in our own ways. He was very much aware of that. He dealt basically with very fundamental materials. Whenever anyone asks me what I learned from Lennie, I have to stop and think for a minute. I think I learned about chords, basic chords, the scales . . . always about the fundamental, theoretical things. And about listening carefully to the music—learn and experience solos by the great jazz musicians. The conversations we had are more difficult to relate, but the intensity of his devotion was what mainly affected everybody, I think. He was almost fanatically intense in his devotion. Having been moved so much by the music he had heard throughout the years—a music basically invented by the great black musicians—I think somewhere along the line he wished to contribute to the music. So there was that kind of motivation, too, in his development.

I think his strong devotion became a problem in many ways. He became very critical in a kind of negative way. A lot of black musicians respected him, I think, but didn't appreciate his criticizing some of them—basically for being commercial or selling out. He was insane about Thelonious Monk, and someone told me that in a radio interview he did shortly before he died he was still saying that Monk was a terrible piano player. Why would he have to do that? So that was an unfortunate part of it. I think Tristano really wanted to be a performer and get that nice contact with the audience—he was very concerned about that—and then something happened. He got afraid, I guess, to go out, or it was too difficult for him as a blind man or whatever, but he decided not to go out anymore and I think that was his undoing. Teaching is not enough. As a supplement to playing it's great, but having to depend on that for a living and for your musical reality it's just not enough—and I think that killed him.

You are a teacher yourself. Do you teach the same way Tristano did?

Well, the things he told me and everybody else . . . and I just read the interview you did with Warne Marsh ten years ago, in which he says that he is basically teaching what he learned from Lennie. Because what we learned are the truths of this music. I'm still saying the same things basically—you gotta do this and you gotta do that in order to learn this. The music has changed into many different areas, and some of these areas I haven't dealt with. I'm still playing basically in the same forms, so that's what I have to talk about because that's what I know best. Tristano was really one of the first to make some kind of methodology out of jazz education, and there's hardly any tribute paid to him in that respect, as far as I know . . .

It was a very dynamic experience every time I worked with or played with Tristano. He really encouraged everyone to play as freely as they could and to open up and blow. On some record, I heard him say "blow" to Warne once. He loved Warne especially, and I can understand that because Warne is a very special musician as you well know. My feeling was that it was a perfect situation, the student-apprenticeship kind of relationship, exactly the way it should be done.

You study and do your lessons, and then you get to play with the teacher. The only problem . . . well, there were a few problems and maybe I should discuss them at this point in time. It might give you an idea why something didn't work if I'm accurate. It was a perfect opportunity for a group to exist and to grow as students with their teacher, and when we played we were equals. It wasn't like he was the teacher. He was the band leader and that's how we thought of him, and when we went out on the road occasionally we were hanging out together like buddies. The music we were playing happened during the very development of bebop, and bebop was becoming accepted as the next music. I remember when Birdland opened, there was a program that listed the history of jazz. Lester Young was on it and Charlie Parker, there was a Dixieland band with some of the best players, and I think Stan Getz was in there some place. And the last band on the program was the Lennie Tristano sextet, and believe me, after listening to all that great music, it was hard to feel like this is where the music is going, folks. We were the avant-garde, you know, and I don't remember being very comfortable that night. It wasn't quite the time for that band to make a real impression because bebop was the thing. Well, the group could have been like a Dave Brubeck thing off the main route, but I think Lennie's idea, just having a band of students, was a large reason why it didn't continue. I think if he at least had had a strong and professional rhythm section, Kenny Clarke and some of the other great players, to help us, things would have worked out differently. Lennie's music is famous for not having had good and imaginative rhythm sections, and that's one of the reasons that we didn't stay together and really become a working group. Well, I think that's all I care to say about it for now . . .

Since the time with Lennie Tristano, you and Warne Marsh have reunited on quite a few occasions, the last time around 1975. Many of us wish you would be able to play together more often. Your styles seem to match so beautifully . . .

That was one of the miracles I was talking about—when two people who are so different in many ways can communicate for a minute about something. That was one of the best ways we could communicate together, and when it was in a context as students with Lennie it was just that. We didn't really communicate too much away from the situation, and that's really the way it has always been. When someone says what you just said, I'm always pleased to know that it happened, that for a moment in life I was able to communicate with someone who I admire very much and make some music. Regrettably we weren't able to do it all through the years for whatever reason, personal or geographical. All I can tell you is that I think Warne is one of the great improvisers of all time, and certainly in years to come the perspective concerning his importance will be more accurate.

Do you feel that your own music has been appreciated the way it should?

I'm overwhelmed at the appreciation I've gotten. I just feel bad about the fact that I can't work too much in my home town, New York City, which is the center of jazz. But neither can Elvin Jones or Clark Terry or anybody. There are hundreds of other guys waiting in line to work those jobs, too. I took my own band to Japan last December and that was a very special feeling for me, to have a good band and play our music. I'm taking that same band with Harold Danko, Rufus Reid, and Al Harewood to Nice in July, and that will be special too. I hope to work with my own band more and more, and the rest of the time I'm more than pleased to be accepted working with many local musicians. Fortunately, there are people interested in jazz in countries like Italy, Germany, and Denmark, and I'm going back to Europe in October this year already.

You worked with Miles Davis in the late '40s and early '50s . . .

Playing with Miles in the late '40s was another special event. To me, it was in the category of playing chamber jazz. Interesting arrangements, and I got an opportunity to play a few solos. My main interest at that time was the things I was doing with Lennie, and it seemed like very familiar music. Last year I played at the Montreal Festival. My band was playing at 11:30 at night and Miles's band was scheduled at 12:30 in the big hall on the other side of the medium-sized hall we were playing in. Our last tune was a composition by George Russell, "Ezz-thetic," which Miles recorded with my sextet in 1951. I told Miles about it the next morning while we were having breakfast, and it was very strange since he's such a different character now and we hadn't really talked for many years. He didn't seem to remember George Russell's composition, and I sang it to him. He looked at me through his dark glasses and said, "Oh, you mean . . ." and sang something to me that I didn't understand at all. I don't know if he was putting me on or if he sang something he just made up at the table.

Your repertoire hasn't changed much over the years. Along with new compositions, you still play the standards you have been playing for quite some years . . .

I'm not interested that much in tunes per se. I'm more interested in approaching familiar materials and getting a new viewpoint on them. That is my particular strangeness, and in my band, when we have time to rehearse, we play some of my new compositions. And I don't know if offhand I can call any tune as good as most of those standards. I mean, I love Wayne Shorter's tunes and they create a new challenge, but I still haven't been able to learn these tunes with the intensity,

I guess, as "Star Eyes" and all those nice tunes. I found this with Charlie Parker and Sonny Rollins and Lennie and Warne and many others. . . . They tended to stay with the same body of things when they performed.

Once you were considered an avant-garde musician, and I think many of us still regard you as that . . .

Well, within the form that I'm functioning in, I try to stay new and renewed, so in that sense I'm not using any new forms. The only thing that was avant-garde about Lennie's situation was the fact that there were a few free pieces. Otherwise, we were just playing standards with a new viewpoint. That term, avant-garde, is used very loosely for any kind of an experiment whether it's valid or not. I feel I'm contemporary within an established form, and I'm satis-fied with that. I might learn something new tomorrow that will bring me on another course. Some of our live performances, when we did some free form pieces with Lennie, I regret they weren't recorded.

How is your musical situation right now?

It's better than ever. As I mentioned, I'm on this European tour right now. I was in Italy for a month, in Paris for a week, and before I came to Denmark I was in Germany for a few days. From here I'm going to England to play with John Taylor, Dave Green, and Trevor Tompkins for a tour around Britain. Also this year I will make a few records, I don't know how many. So I would say that this is the best year for me in many respects, in terms of being able to work at my music, and I think next year will be even better. Back in New York I have my own band, which is not a permanent band, but my nonet is a thing of the past. The next time I do a thing like that again will be when I'm thinking orchestrally, and I'm not thinking that way now. For the time being I prefer a small improvising orchestra.

Gunther Schuller sent me a piece that he wrote for saxophone and or-chestra, but I wasn't really interested in playing it. The orchestration is very modern, very interesting, some of the most interesting saxophone orchestra-tion I've heard. I do want to play with a large orchestra, and I do want to create some music with a composer because I haven't been able to do that yet. In fact, it's in the process of being done right now. There's a French violin player named Pierre Blanchard, who is in New York now, and I kind of commissioned him to write a string quartet piece that will be recorded when it's finished. And David Baker, we talked about him writing a twenty-minute piece. Tony Baker, my friend in New Zealand, is writing twenty minutes of music that I will record for the radio and hopefully, Sonet will put a record out on it. In July I'll be recording with a thirty-five-voice female choir that Italian pianist

Guido Manusardi has written some music for. It's a group of women, none of whom can read music, from his hometown, Milan, and he plays their parts and they learn it by ear, and that's the best way. He has written arrangements of "All the Things You Are" and "Summertime," a piece by Kodaly, and some of his own compositions, a variety of things. He is going to record the group in June, and then I'll come in with the rhythm section and overdub. Those kinds of things are beginning to open up for me finally. I have been very impressed and inspired by the achievements of Wynton Marsalis. He does what he is doing so well, and he also has the power to name his projects. I mean, I've been playing all these years and I have wanted to play with a big orchestra, but that's very expensive and no one was willing to really invest that money in me.

I also wish to say that I have been involved in Scientology since 1973, and that basically to me means the writings of L. Ron Hubbard. His writings have been very inspirational to me. Chick Corea actually was the one who introduced me to L. Ron Hubbard and his writings. I find Chick right now is one of the nicest, cleanest, and most creative people I know. He has just straightened up his act, and where he did everything before, he is now just an inspired man.

What do you listen to at home?

I've been enjoying listening to some tapes I have with Joe Henderson lately, and I've been enjoying very much Wayne Shorter's new album, *Atlantis.* I have the record, and I have a live performance of the band that I recorded from the radio, where they stretch out the material. If that were the level of pop music, we would have a much different ballgame. I've always enjoyed listening to Bach and I frequently listen to Bartok. Some of the works of the Polish composer Lutosławski have impressed me very much. I don't listen too much to pop music—that's still an area that's last on my list, and I feel it's about time I became kind of knowledgeable about. . . . I mean, I don't even really know Stevie Wonder's music. Most of the musicians I talk with know that music very well, and I feel like I'm missing something. I just can't fit it into my schedule somehow. We have priorities, you know. There are so many fine improvisers that I don't know them all, because if I have an hour or so to listen to music, I usually put the best players on.

I also listen to my own records, and not only do I listen to them more and more but I finally decided that it's very important in my understanding of this whole process. We must get very familiar with the great solos of other players, and we also must get familiar with our own solos. We must sing and copy and write down our own solos, and I'm gradually doing that more and more, something I never really did before. In order to keep things in perspective, we must pay that much respect to our own efforts.

· 16 ·

Pierre Dørge

Entirely self-taught, Pierre Dørge (b. 1946) started playing guitar when he was 12 and soon won amateur contests with his quintet. From the late '60s, he often collaborated with John Tchicai and played various styles of rock music. In 1980 he founded the twelve-piece New Jungle Orchestra, which has since been touring most of the world presenting mainly Dørge's own music, which mixes inspirations from Duke Ellington and Ornette Coleman as well as Balinese and West African music into a synthesis that never loses its basic jazz flavor. The New Jungle Orchestra was the official Danish state ensemble from 1993 through '96.

To be a band leader, musician, composer, and music teacher are all parts of the same process. To prepare for and teach your students is similar to composing and arranging, and sometimes my students perform music that I later introduce to my New Jungle Orchestra. In the last few years, *that* band has been my main thing musically. I never imagined that the band would ever be internationally known to the extent it is today. Now and then I have to pinch my arm and ask myself if I'm dreaming. . . . All of this has happened because of the records we have done for SteepleChase, and it is extremely difficult for me to explain the reason for our success or whatever you want to call it. The SteepleChase records were distributed in the States as well as in Japan and all over Europe, and our music was played on radio stations and reached audiences who found the music interesting and different. The musicians in the band are totally dedicated, and as for myself I try to get *my* music, *my* musical ideas out of them, and in a way that is right for the musicians I work with. My music is quite open, and it is very important that my musicians are creative, that we are together in making the music happen when it is being performed. I have learned to be more authoritative than before, though, and have found out that this is *my* band, and that I have some ideas I want to have expressed. John Tchicai and I write most of the music for the band, and we also play music by, for instance, Ellington and

Previously published in *Coda*, August 1987

the Danish composer Helmer Nørgaard. John once said that he and I belong to the same tribe, and actually I consider him my teacher. We started working together in 1969 when I was a member of his Cadentia Nova Danica. That band recorded for Joachim-Ernst Berendt in 1969, and if everything works out we will be playing at Berendt's festival in Germany in June 1987 with the New Jungle Orchestra.

I formed the New Jungle Orchestra in 1980 together with another Danish jazz musician, saxophonist Simon Spang-Hanssen. We wanted to hear our compositions arranged for and played by a large ensemble, and that's what we did at first. I work differently now and direct my efforts more towards a specific recording project or concert, considering what music we have that can be used and where we wish to compose, and arrange something new. I may have a theme I want to use, and I try to find out who is going to be featured as soloist on that particular piece. Then I arrange the composition with the soloist or soloists in mind. Unfortunately, the next time we meet, in the spring of 1987, we will have to reduce the size of the band, and that of course has to do with economy. It is simply not possible to get enough jobs with a full-size band. We hope to go to Canada and the States in the summer of 1987, and we just can't travel with fifteen musicians. Therefore, some of the members have to leave the band.

Within the band there is a beautiful understanding and respect among the young musicians and the older, more experienced players like Hugo Rasmussen and John Tchicai. Hugo is respected for the tradition he represents, and John for all his musical conquests. In return they respect the newcomers for bringing fresh ideas into the band. When we play at the Montmartre in Copenhagen, we play for 500 people at the most, but apparently there is a greater interest in our way of playing abroad. In Germany, for instance, there is a big audience for our music. We have also played in Poland, and I have played in Hungary with the group Thermænius, and in both countries we experienced large and very attentive audiences who really took in all the musical details and showed an enormous interest in getting acquainted with music from the western world. To them that music is like a symbol of freedom—be it or not! We have played at one concert in the States so far—at the Chicago Jazz Festival in 1986—and I felt the same kind of interest. It was quite overwhelming to play for 60,000 people at an outdoor concert, one of those situations where it is hard to understand what is really happening; it's like a dream in a way. To get lost in the music, to go into a sort of trance, may also happen when you play for a smaller audience because it doesn't really matter if you play for 60,000 or fourteen people. Because of the international publicity, the interest in my music has also grown in my own country. Here in Copenhagen, a new radio station, Radio

Jazz, is being established in 1987 and I think it will stimulate the interest of jazz. Radio Denmark plays a good deal of jazz in many of its programs, but the information about the music—if any at all—is too often superficial. Everything considered, I experience an increasing interest in jazz—especially when I'm in a teaching situation.

It is a sign of the times that the young musicians are more aware of the jazz tradition than musicians were, say, twenty years ago. The education many young people get today also makes them more conscious of the jazz roots. Many of them learn to play within the bop tradition, while there is no system really as far as teaching free jazz is concerned. Free jazz, as we call it, is more open than bop, but at the same time it may be very limited in terms of expression. In other words, the young generation can learn to play bop, study it, and sort of grow up with it along with the music of Miles Davis and Wayne Shorter of the '60s. I was very surprised when I was in Hungary and visited their jazz institute. On the day I was there, they had a class of traditional jazz and a big band was rehearsing Joe Zawinul's composition "Birdland," while some saxophone players were rehearsing a transcribed solo by John Tchicai—one of the solos from his recordings with the New York Contemporary Five, as far as I can remember. I have had a few lessons with Ornette Coleman, and what I learned from him were some very simple things, but things I have used a lot. I have been and still am fascinated by Ornette's music, but when I started playing I was more influenced by artists like Sonny Rollins and Charles Mingus. Mingus's method of conducting his musicians in a concert situation has also inspired me, and Mingus was—like I am myself—inspired by Duke Ellington and his tradition. Another major inspiration is Gil Evans. The New Jungle Orchestra is often compared with the Vienna Art Orchestra from Austria and Willem Breuker Kollektief from Holland.

I heard Albert Ayler a few times back in the '60s. He turned up a lot of places in Copenhagen at that time, and he wasn't always very welcome. It is through his records, though, that I have really become familiar with his music, which I have listened a lot to. Tchicai is also very much into Ayler's music. Another musician who impressed me deeply was Eric Dolphy, whom I also heard in Copenhagen. I recall a bass clarinet solo that lasted, I think, more than a half hour. The place was crowded and people were sitting on tables and windowsills. When he wasn't playing any tones on his instrument, the place was so quiet that you might hear a pin drop. It was one of my great musical moments. Around the same time, Don Cherry was in Copenhagen with the New York Contemporary Five, and Don's way of arranging music is something I use in my music today—the loosely suggested themes on top of a flowing rhythm. His way of creating themes and his phrasing interested me, and I try to use some of his ideas in my own guitar playing. Among guitarists, I am particularly inspired by people like Django Reinhardt, especially by his tone and vibrato, and Frank Zappa. I also listen to John Scofield, John Abercrombie, Pat Metheny, and other contemporaries, but the way I play is different from theirs. Actually, I don't think I have heard anybody play the guitar the way I do it.

In addition to my work with the New Jungle Orchestra, I am busy in other musical areas. People ask me to compose music for other ensembles. I find it hard to write that way, and the music doesn't always turn out the way I had thought it should sound. I prefer to create music at the moment it is being performed. During my travels in West Africa, I listened to the local music, and in my own music I have tried to blend jazz elements and the ethnic music of Africa. In the oldest jazz, as we know it, there are not many African elements like polyrhythms, but as early as in the late '20s we see African elements in Duke Ellington's music, for instance. I have also been, and still am, deeply inspired by the music of the East. This year I visited Nepal to listen to the music of the Tibetan monks. I try to absorb music and sounds from everywhere and to learn from it.

My newest record is *Canoe*, recorded in August this year with two of the members of the New Jungle Orchestra: saxophonist Morten Carlsen, with whom I have played since 1971, and my wife, Irene Becker, who plays keyboards and is a composer as well. We will continue working in that trio format with the possibility of adding other musicians, the first being percussionist Marilyn Mazur, who is featured on the album. The record shows another side of our music, a more ballad-like, airy, and contemplative type of music—a contrast to the music of the New Jungle Orchestra, you might say.

· 17 ·

John Tchicai

John Tchicai (b. 1936) grew up in Århus, Denmark, where he played violin from the age of ten and clarinet and alto saxophone from the age of sixteen. In 1962 he played at festivals in Helsinki, where he met Archie Shepp, and the same year he moved to New York. During his time in the U.S. he worked with the New York Contemporary Five and the New York Art Quartet and recorded with, among others, Albert Ayler and John Coltrane. Back in Copenhagen in 1966, he was the leading force in Cadentia Nova Danica and was for a number of years always on the move, living in Germany, Holland, Switzerland, and Denmark, playing with a host of free-jazz and avant-garde musicians and also devoting much time to teaching. Since the early '90s he has been living in California, visiting Denmark regularly, and working with Pierre Dørge and the New Jungle Orchestra, among others. At 71, he is still a musical explorer.

I grew up in Århus, Denmark's second largest city, and listened a lot to the radio. In the evenings when my father was at work, I took over the radio and listened mostly to the American stations in Germany and AFN, the American Forces Network. I also listened to the jazz program on Voice of America. It's a long time ago, but I think Gerry Mulligan and Duke Ellington were some of the first names I heard. Shortly after the war, I started going to Sweden to buy records, 78s, as it was difficult to get any records in Denmark. One of the first records I got was with Moe Koffman, and otherwise I just bought what I could find. Later on I purchased records from a Danish mail-order company run by Ole Vestergaard in Brande. There was also live jazz in Århus, and as far as I remember one of the first things I heard was a concert with Lionel Hampton and his band. Another musician I heard was my half brother, Kaj Timmermann, with the Harlem Kiddies, and on the local scene I listened to people like Louis Hjulmand, Hugo Hjulmand, and Mogens Lauridsen, who played vibraphone, clarinet, and piano respectively. So I was a member of a small jazz community before I started playing myself. I was almost twenty before I started playing alto saxophone. I had several teachers in Århus, and later on I went to the conservatory and stud-

Previously published in *Coda*, August 1988

ied clarinet for two or three years. I didn't like it too much, and at that time there was no such thing as a jazz education. After Århus, I went to Copenhagen and was drafted into the Danish Navy. In Copenhagen, one of my teachers was Ib Glindemann, who will be remembered for his big band.

In Copenhagen, I met quite a lot of young players and even formed my own quintet. Some of the musicians who first influenced me were Lee Konitz and the saxophone players in Lionel Hampton's band—Anthony Ortega, for one. Others I listened to were Johnny Hodges and Benny Carter. What fascinated me in Konitz' playing was partly his smooth sound, and a certain calmness and something restful in the sound. The total language of his music was very interesting. Konitz' playing has changed over the years, but he's still one of my favorites. I heard him last year in Copenhagen. On that particular night he was playing standards mostly, but at my request he played Thelonious Monk's composition "Well You Needn't" and one of the things John Coltrane used to play. When I lived in New York, I went to Lee's house in Hackensack a couple of times to play. When I came to Copenhagen, I heard many of the visiting American musicians who, in those days, quite often would play with some of the Danish musicians after their concerts on jam sessions. Some of the Danish musicians I would hear were Max Brüel, Jørgen Ryg, Bent Axen, and William Schiøpffe. As for myself, I was at that time—and probably still am—considered an outsider. My style of playing was different from theirs, and I think they felt my playing was not educated enough and that I started to express myself too early. When we played at Vingaarden, a very famous club at that time, we sometimes would have disagreements. In those days it was more common to sit in, and some people could sit in and others could not. . . . That's the way it was. When Max Brüel and I had our group and played at Vingaarden every Sunday afternoon for a long period of time, I think we had an enthusiastic audience and created a nice atmosphere. The same was true when we played Monday nights at the old Montmartre. I remember Torben Ulrich being one of the first critics to write something that made me feel a kind of support and appreciation. That was one thing that helped me continue and not to be discouraged by too much negativism from other musicians.

In 1962 I went to New York City and stayed there for almost four years. At my request, my wife applied for and got a job at the Danish Consulate in New York because I wanted to go there, to meet the American musicians in their own country and to develop my own playing. I had met several young American musicians over here, like Albert Ayler, and I felt it would be much more interesting over there. I thought Ayler had a fantastic, expressive sound and that he was very different. I didn't find his playing ugly or anything. We also played together when he came to Copenhagen and sat in at Vingaarden.

Unfortunately I didn't tape those encounters. When I came to New York, we were together very often and he was always around sitting in and listening to the young musicians. This summer, when I was in New York with the New Jungle Orchestra, they had an Albert Ayler birthday celebration and played twenty-four hours of interviews and music by Ayler on the radio. I was also invited to talk about him, but as I had another engagement I couldn't make it.

New York in the early '60s meant a lot of activity, and right away I got a lot of invitations to play. In the beginning it was mostly practicing, rehearsing, and small benefit concerts. There was a lot of energy and enthusiasm among the young musicians. I remember playing with Bill Dixon, Steve Lacy, Roswell Rudd, and Archie Shepp, and at the Half Note I sat in with Coltrane for the first time. A little later, in 1965, I recorded with him—the Ascension session for Impulse. The idea of bringing several young musicians into the studio could have been a joint idea of Coltrane and the producer, Bob Thiele. I was there, Marion Brown and Dewey Johnson were there, Archie Shepp, Freddie Hubbard, and Coltrane's regular group. Recording with Coltrane was in a way a dream come true and I felt things were going the right way. I was very honored to be invited to play and record with Coltrane. He just brought to the studio a few sketches and he told us his ideas, but he gave us a lot of freedom to solo. Coltrane was like a mentor; he helped a lot of people. I was very fortunate because at the same time I was playing and recording with my own group. I even had a job as a cook at a Danish restaurant, and my wife had her job. But it was hard times for a lot of the young musicians, and Coltrane helped many of them. I stayed most of the time within that small circle, but I remember hearing Woody Herman's band a couple of times at a place on Times Square. I went to Harlem, also, to Small's Paradise, where I heard some blues singers and some other nice music. My own group, the New York Contemporary Five, made some recordings for Storyville and for Philips. The group was originally an idea of Shepp and myself. Don Cherry was in the group, but we felt obligated to Bill Dixon, who had taken us into his group and had always treated us nicely. However, when we got a chance to go to Europe with the Contemporary Five, we felt it would be better to take Don. I think Dixon was very disappointed because of our decision. As it turned out, we might have done better with Dixon, because Don gave us a lot of trouble because of his personal problems. Sometimes when we were to play here in Copenhagen, we just couldn't find him. The same thing was true with our drummer, J. C. Moses. So it wasn't always easy to be a band leader getting established and facing problems like those on top of all other problems. The New York Contemporary Five existed for about two years, and I think that the group was pretty successful and the recordings we made were, too. As a matter of fact I have just written to one of those companies, Philips in Holland, asking about my royalties because I haven't received any for quite some time. I know they have recently released some of that music in Japan.

I left New York after about four years, and left a hectic scene with a lot of partying and pot smoking. My wife and I felt we needed to go back, but I learned a lot in the States. I came back to Denmark in 1966 and came back to almost no activity at all. In the beginning I didn't work too much, and around that time I performed one of the first happenings here in Denmark. It was in the canteen of Radio Denmark. I dropped a tray full of glasses, I made a speech, and I broke my saxophone. . . . I was very mad at that time, and the happening was my way of attracting attention, to protest the fact that young jazz musicians were not given enough opportunity to play their music. It helped! We made a long series of concerts for the radio with a large group, Cadentia Nova Danica. That group also participated in several arrangements that had a very experimental concept. Society at that time was very open to new things, and we got many opportunities to perform. I remember, for instance, one thing we did at the Montmartre with two Japanese doing a mime act, things like that. I still find it interesting to combine music with other arts, and in countries like Germany and Holland I find that many people are interested in that kind of project. Around that time, the late '60s, I got interested in yoga and was doing a lot of exercises and meditation. At one point I started to go into seclusion, trying to achieve a more stable lifestyle. I had a job as a teacher for singers for three years. I stayed at the school most of the time, and only played occasionally. I was also conducting a small saxophone workshop at a music school. I still do vocals with the New Jungle Orchestra, as well as on one of my latest albums, *Put Up the Fight*.

Before I joined the Jungle Orchestra, five or six years ago I did a lot of work with a trio called Strange Brothers, and even traveled in Germany with the group. That was my start getting out of seclusion, in the mid-'70s, and getting back to the jazz scene. I still work with two of the musicians from Strange Brothers, the bassist Peter Danstrup and the drummer Ole Rømer. The tenor player from Strange Brothers—Simon Spang-Hanssen, who is now living in Paris—was involved in forming the New Jungle Orchestra with Pierre Dørge. I joined the Jungle Orchestra a little while after it was formed and have been with the band ever since. The orchestra played Canada and the States last year, and we had a good time and a beautiful reception. We played every night, and in Washington we performed at an open-air festival and got a chance to listen to some of the other artists at the festival. One was Buck Hill, known as the Postman, and another was Andrew White, who played with his group. I also met an alto player called C-Sharp, a very fine player in the Charlie Parker tradition. Not too long ago I met Archie Shepp when I played with the bassist Johnny Dyani in a club in Northampton in Massachusetts. Shepp was living nearby and came to hear us, and it was good to see him and talk with him. We were also in the area where Roswell Rudd lives, but I didn't see him and somebody told me that he gave up playing completely. I hope it's not true.

I travel a lot and play in many different connections, and for the Danes it's pretty hard to keep track. Actually, I play more outside Denmark than in the country. My base is partly here and partly in Switzerland. Many of the younger jazz musicians have become interested in older forms of playing. I think I'm like that myself—I like to go back and find material from earlier periods of time.

The record I made for SteepleChase in 1977, *Real Tchicai*, with Niels-Henning Ørsted Pedersen and Pierre Dørge, I think gives a good example of my playing. So does the recent album I have already mentioned, *Put Up the Fight*. Johnny Dyani is on the new album, and through the years I have played a lot with Johnny. He is African, and I have always been very interested in African music. My father was from Africa, and I have played in several of the West African states with local musicians. A couple of records will be coming out on which you will hear me play with African musicians . . .

Name Index

About the Author

Roland Baggenæs was born and grew up in Denmark, and as a teenager and schoolboy he was turned on to jazz around 1950, mainly from listening to the radio—at that time especially an invaluable source when it came to education and entertainment. The weekly jazz program on Radio Denmark, and the broadcasts from AFN (American Forces Network) in Germany and Voice of America, all stimulated and increased his interest. Later on, when records became available, he was able to listen and study more thoroughly and was intrigued by the music of such artists as Lee Konitz, Warne Marsh, Thelonious Monk, Sonny Rollins, John Coltrane, Miles Davis, and the two saxophonists Charlie Parker and Lester Young—whom he considers the greatest improvisers. After leaving school he was trained and worked in Danish banks. In the 1960s he attended a Danish teachers' college and obtained his degree in 1969, majoring in English and Danish literature. He also took up writing for local newspapers and soon concentrated on writing about jazz, the music that has been and still is a lifelong passion. He wrote reviews, articles, and interviews for Danish newspapers and magazines and produced several jazz programs for Radio Denmark. In 1986 he wrote a number of biographies for the Danish "Politikens Jazzleksikon" and, in 1988, biographies for *The New Grove Dictionary of Jazz*. From 1976 to 1991, he was jazz editor at the Danish newspaper *Jyllands-Posten*, and from 1972 to 1992 he contributed to the Canadian jazz magazine *Coda*. After a few visits to West Africa, he made The Gambia his home in 2004. He is currently working on a book about the life and people in The Gambia.